Young Students Encyclopedia

7

Ear

Federal Bureau

Funk & Wagnalls, Inc.
New York, N.Y.

Acknowledgements

All photographs supplied by Armando Curcio Editore, SpA, except the following:

Arp Instruments—page 992.

Bell Telephone Laboratories—page 993.

The Bettmann Archive, Inc.—pages 1003 bottom, 1030.

Jean F. Blashfield—page 1023.

Bonneville Power Administration—page 987.

Kristi Brown—page 1093 top.

Bureau of Indian Affairs—page 970 bottom, 1038.

Cadillac Motor Car Division/General Motors Corporation—page 1019 top.

Canadian Government Travel Bureau Photo—frontispiece.

Coast and Geodetic Survey Official Photograph—page 954.

Department of Transport, Canada—page 1066.

DICTIONARY OF AMERICAN PORTRAITS BY CIRKER AND CIRKER, Dover Publications, Inc., New York, Reprinted through permission of the publisher—pages 944 (courtesy Mercaldo Archives), 1009 (Engraving by J. A. J. Wilcox).

E. I. du Pont de Nemours & Company—page 1068.

Dorothy M. Evans—page 1077.

Federal Bureau of Investigation—page 1096.

Florida Department of Commerce—page 1055.

The Ford Foundation—pages 968, 974 bottom.

General Electric—page 985.

Thomas Gillett—page 1000.

The Joseph Mordecai Hirschmann Collection, courtesy Leah Read Barkowitz—page 955 bottom.

High Voltage Engineering Corporation—page 1014.

Russell F. Hogeland—pages 1012, 1080, 1087 bottom left.

Institute for Parapsychology—page 1071.

Charles R. Knight/The Chicago Field Museum of Natural History—pages 949, 950 top, 950 bottom, 953, 1058, 1059.

Library of Congress—pages 967 top, 996 top, 1002 bottom, 1035 left, 1054, 1081 top.

Lick Observatory—page 958 top.

Make-up by Max Factor—page 1087 center left.

Florence Mallet—page 966.

Don Meredith—page 983 top.

Mary E. A. Mitchell—pages 962 bottom, 969, 1061.

NASA—pages 945, 979 bottom, 1067.

National Air and Space Museum, Smithsonian Institution—page 943.

National Gallery of Art, Washington, D.C.—pages 1003 top, 1035 right, 1042 bottom, 1043 center.

New Jersey Department of Conservation and Economic Development—page 962 top.

Otis Elevator—pages 1001, 1002 top.

Overseas National Airways—page 1087 center right.

J-L. Ray-C.E.P.A.—page 1073 top.

Smithsonian Institution—page 970 top.

Smithsonian Institution, Freer Gallery of Art, Washington, D.C.—page 1010 bottom.

Southwestern Power Administration—page 985 top.

Trans World Airlines Photo—pages 1050 top, 1050 bottom, 1051 bottom.

United Press International Photo—page 981.

United States Capitol Historical Society—page 1063 bottom.

United States Department of Agriculture Photo—pages 1037 bottom, 1073 bottom left, 1073 bottom right, 1081 bottom, 1082 left, 1082 right, 1083 top left, 1083 top right, 1091.

United States Steel—page 1021.

Cathleen L. Yordi—page 1044.

Maps from the Pictograph Corporation.

The fun of the fair is always sure to attract a large crowd. Here, a colorful sculpture of fascinating shapes stands in front of the big wheel, a fairground favorite. (See FAIR.)

EAR People who use matchsticks, hairpins, or other small, sharp objects to clean out wax from their ears may do a lot of damage. A wad of cotton on a stick can be used for this purpose, but don't dig in with it. If something gets stuck in your ear, let the doctor get it out!

The ear is the organ not only of hearing but also of balance and position. The ear of humans and other mammals has three principal parts: the outer ear, the middle ear, and the inner ear. All play a special role in hearing.

The *outer ear* is the part of your ear that you can see. It includes the outer ear canal, which leads into the head. At the back end of the canal is the *eardrum*. The eardrum is a taut membrane, something like the head of a drum. The eardrum separates the outer ear from the middle ear. The function of the outer ear is to collect sound waves and carry them to the eardrum. When sound waves in the air hit the eardrum, they cause it to vibrate (move rapidly back and forth).

The *middle ear* is a small, air-filled chamber. It contains three little bones named because of their shapes—the *hammer,* the *anvil,* and the *stirrup.* These bones work together to carry the vibrations from the eardrum into the inner ear. The hammer touches the eardrum, the anvil touches the hammer, and the stirrup touches the anvil. The eardrum vibrates in response to sounds, and its vibrations cause the ear bones to move. This movement is carried to the inner ear through an opening called the *oval window.*

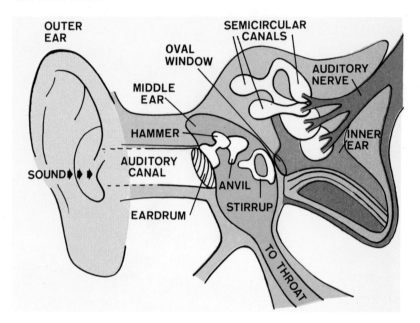

The chamber of the middle ear is connected to the throat by a narrow tube that leads to the nose. The tube keeps the air pressure in the middle ear chamber the same as the air pressure outside. A person's ears get plugged up and may hurt when he rides into a railroad tunnel, or when he is in an airplane that is coming down for a landing. This happens because the pressure inside the ear is greater than outside. The tube quickly corrects this, and the pain goes away. You can help equalize the pressure by swallowing several times, or by covering your nose, closing your mouth, and trying to breathe out. If the pressure difference were not corrected, your eardrum could soon burst, like a balloon with too much air in it.

The *inner ear* is a fluid-filled, spiral passage that looks much like a snail shell. A membrane winds down this passage, almost but not quite dividing it into two complete parts. This membrane contains rows of special cells called *hair cells,* which are connected to the *auditory* (hearing) nerves.

The rapid back-and-forth movements of the earbones in the

middle ear are transmitted through the oval window to the fluid in the inner ear. The fluid moves, pushing the membrane that runs through the spiral passage and moving the hair cells on the membrane. The vibration of the hair cells causes the auditory nerves to send impulses to the brain, which interprets them into sounds we recognize.

In the inner ear is another organ, called the *semicircular canals,* the organ of our sense of balance. These canals form approximate right angles with each other. Two are placed vertically (up-and-down), and one is placed horizontally (side-to-side). The canals are lined with sensitive hairs and filled with fluid. When the head and body move, the fluid also moves, but not quite so quickly. As the movement bends the hairs in the canals, nerves send messages to the brain. If you spin very quickly and stop suddenly, the fluid continues to move for a short time. The nerve cells send confusing messages to your brain, and you suddenly feel dizzy. The dizziness ends when the fluid stops moving.

Without the semicircular canals, simple tasks like walking would be extremely difficult, if not impossible. And the canals also provide a sense of position, or *orientation.* Without this, you would even have difficulty knowing whether you were standing up, sitting down, lying on your back, or lying on your side.

ALSO READ: BRAIN, HEARING, NERVOUS SYSTEM, SENSE ORGAN, SPECIAL EDUCATION.

EARHART, AMELIA (1898-1937) Amelia Earhart believed women should be given the same chances as men in any job. But she also believed that women should earn their right to work by doing their jobs as well as or better than men. As a young girl, she saved newspaper stories about women who had succeeded in difficult professions.

Amelia was born in Atchison, Kansas. She went to college for a while, but she quit her studies to go into one of the toughest new professions—aviation. She wanted to become a professional pilot. She learned to fly a plane, and she studied weather, navigation, how an airplane flies, and all other things a pilot must know.

In 1932 she became the first woman to fly alone across the Atlantic Ocean. She was awarded the Distinguished Flying Cross for this achievement. In 1935, she was the first person to make a solo flight across the Pacific Ocean from Hawaii to California, and she set a speed record flying from Mexico City to New Jersey. She was given the Harmon Trophy, one of the nation's highest aviation awards.

Miss Earhart died in 1937, when she and her navigator, Fred Noonan, were lost in their plane over the Pacific. They were

▼*Amelia Earhart, American flyer.*

trying to make the first flight around the world at the equator. Neither they nor their plane were ever found.

Amelia Earhart was a true pioneer. During her brief life, she won the respect of many people all over the world.

ALSO READ: AVIATION.

EARP, WYATT (1848-1929) Stories are often told about famous people. Sometimes these stories leave out things that happened and add things that did not happen. Some stories are more legendary (made up) than factual (true). The story of Wyatt Earp is a good example of this.

The legendary Wyatt Earp was a hero of the American West. He was a deputy marshal in Tombstone, Arizona. The stories say he was a brave, honest man who fought against outlaws and brought law and order to the frontier. The stories praise his most famous gunfight—the gunfight at the O.K. Corral on October 26, 1881—in which Wyatt Earp, his two brothers, and Doc Holliday shot it out with the Clanton gang.

Wyatt Earp really was a marshal. But he was also a boaster, a bully, and a cheat at cards. He used his lawman's badge to take advantage of other people. He had many enemies. He killed his enemies and then said that they had been breaking the law. This is what many believe really happened at the O.K. Corral.

ALSO READ: PIONEER LIFE, WESTWARD MOVEMENT.

▲*Wyatt Earp, lawman of the West whose exploits became legend.*

EARTH The Earth, the planet on which we live, is the third planet from the sun. It is a ball of rock and iron a little more than 7,900 miles through the middle. The Earth is slightly flattened at the North and South poles. The distance from the North Pole to the equator is a little longer than from the equator to the South Pole. Also, the Earth bulges at the equator. But if you were far out in space and could see the whole Earth, it would look like a perfect ball. The flattening and bulging are too small to see.

On Earth's Surface

Mountain climbers take weeks to climb the highest mountains. The tallest mountain, Mount Everest, rises a little more than 5½ miles above the level of the sea. This is a very small rise when compared to the size of the whole Earth. If you were in a rocket near the moon, you would not be able to see Mount Everest at all. You might be able to see the huge continent of Asia, but even that would look very small from so far away.

Water covers nearly three-quarters of the Earth's surface. Almost all of this water makes up the oceans. Some parts of the oceans are seven miles deep, but the average depth is two miles. Although the oceans seem to be vast and deep, they are only a thin film of water on the Earth's surface.

◀A spectacular photograph of Earth taken from a quarter of a million miles away by the crew of Apollo 10. The west coast of North America can be seen. The remaining land mass is covered by clouds.

An envelope of gases, called the *atmosphere,* or air, surrounds the Earth. Oxygen, nitrogen, and carbon dioxide are some of the gases found in the atmosphere. People, animals, and plants need the gases to live.

One-fourth of the Earth's surface is land. Sand or soil covers much of it. The part of the soil in which crops grow is rarely more than 20 inches deep. The materials beneath the soil—clay, silt, and others—are usually not many feet deep, but may extend as much as several hundred feet down to solid rock. About one-fifth of the land, including Antarctica and parts of Canada, Alaska, Siberia, and Greenland, is always covered by ice.

The very thin coverings of air, soil, and water—from the bottom of the sea to the top of the thickest part of the atmosphere—compose a very narrow band on and above the Earth's surface. All living things exist within this region, the *biosphere.*

Under the Surface

Three thick layers of material—called the crust, the mantle, and the core—lie under the Earth's thin surface. The outermost layer of the Earth is a *crust* of rock. The crust is only three miles thick in some places under the ocean. Beneath the continents, it may be 35 miles thick. The average thickness of the crust is 20 miles.

The crust changes constantly. The crust and the very top part of Earth's next layer, the mantle, are divided into huge sections, called *plates.* The dividing lines between plates are areas of earthquake activity. The plates slide across the mantle, very slowly. The movement of the plates causes what scientists call

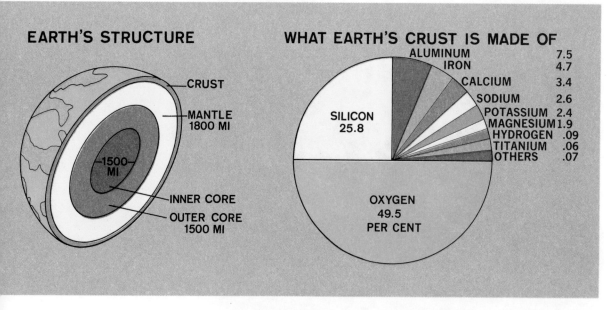

EARTH'S STRUCTURE

CRUST

MANTLE
1800 MI

1500 MI

INNER CORE

OUTER CORE
1500 MI

WHAT EARTH'S CRUST IS MADE OF

ALUMINUM	7.5
IRON	4.7
CALCIUM	3.4
SODIUM	2.6
POTASSIUM	2.4
MAGNESIUM	1.9
HYDROGEN	.09
TITANIUM	.06
OTHERS	.07

SILICON
25.8

OXYGEN
49.5
PER CENT

continental drift—very slow movement, about an inch every year, of Earth's continents.

The movement of the plates, over hundreds of millions of years, has also built up Earth's mountains. The plates sometimes crash into each other. The Himalaya Mountains of Asia were formed when the plate carrying India and the plate carrying Asia crashed. Other mountains have been formed when a plate slid into a deep trench (hole) in the ocean floor. The slipping of the plate disturbs the Earth's surface. In places, layers of the rock that form the crust pile up and mountains are born. The Rocky, Coastal, Cascade, and Sierra Nevada mountain ranges along North America's west coast were all formed in this way.

At the same time that mountains are rising, they are being worn down by the action of running water, blowing wind, and freezing and heating. This wearing away is called *erosion*. Even the highest mountains can erode, if given enough time. Many times in the long history of the Earth, whole mountain chains have been worn down to sea level.

Below the crust is the *mantle*. Like the crust, the mantle is made up of rock. The temperature of the mantle is so great —from 2,000 degrees near the crust to 4,000 degrees at its lowest boundary—that the rock of the mantle is not completely rigid. The rock of the mantle can move when great force is applied to it for a long time. The tremendous pressure caused by the weight of the Earth's surface works with the high temperatures of the mantle to keep the rock from becoming firm. The mantle extends 1,800 miles toward the center of the Earth, ending where the Earth's core begins.

The Earth's *core* is divided into two sections. The *outer core*

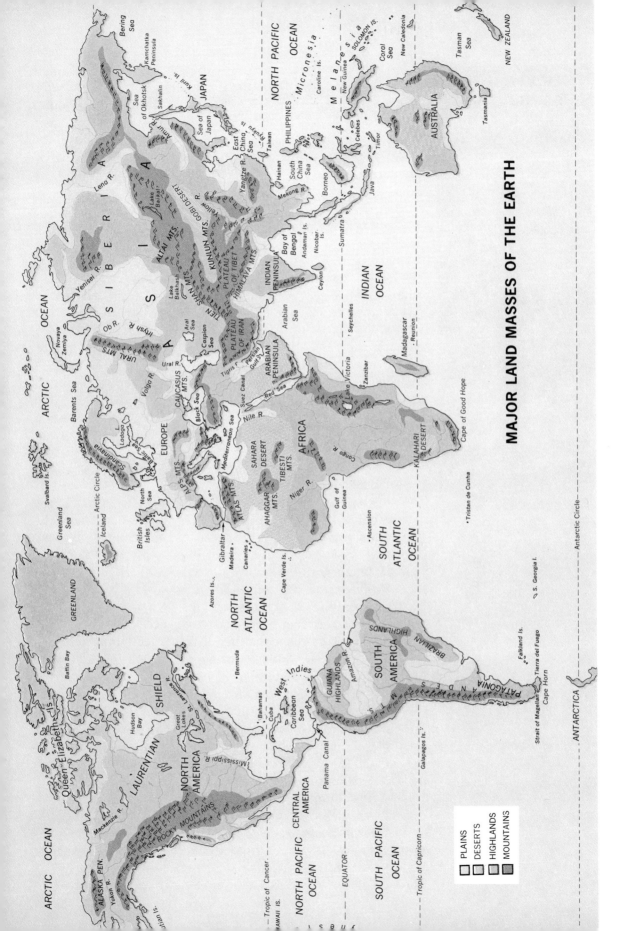

MAJOR LAND MASSES OF THE EARTH

PLAINS
DESERTS
HIGHLANDS
MOUNTAINS

EARTH FACTS

Diameter between North and
South poles . .7,900 miles
Diameter through the equator
. . . . 7,927 miles
Distance around equator
(circumference)
. . . . 24,830 miles
Area of surface . . . .
196,950,000 square miles
Land area . . . .
57,469,928 square miles
Water area . . . .
139,480,841 square miles
Volume . . . .
259,000 million cubic miles
Mass (or weight) . . . .
6,592 million million
million tons
Mass of earth compared to
mass of sun . 1/332,488
Density 5.52
(5.52 x weight
of water of equal volume)
Weight of atmosphere . . . .
5,000 million million tons
Deepest chasm in crust . . .
Marianas Trench:
36,198 feet
Highest part of crust . . . .
Mt. Everest: 29,028 feet

is about 1,500 miles thick, and it probably is made up of molten iron. The *inner core* is a sphere 1,500 miles in diameter. It is probably made up of solid iron, nickel, and cobalt. Scientists really do not know very much about Earth's mantle and core. What they do know, they have learned by studying how earthquake energy moves through the Earth. Scientists will know much more about Earth's inner parts when men are able to drill holes through the crust to the mantle.

Measuring the Earth

The ancient Greeks knew the shape of the Earth. They understood that an eclipse of the moon is caused by the Earth's shadow on the moon. They saw that the shadow was *always* circular as the sun moved in its path around the Earth. (Most Greeks thought the sun moved around the Earth, not the Earth around the sun.) They reasoned that only a sphere could always cast a circular shadow. Therefore, the Earth must be a sphere.

Prove to yourself how the Greeks reasoned. Get an egg, a small juice can, a ball, and a flashlight. Shine the flashlight on the wall. Can you hold the egg in a position that will cause it to have a circular shadow? When you have found this position, move the source of light. What happens to the shape of the shadow? Next, use the can instead of the egg. Finally, use the ball. Can you find a position in which the ball will NOT cast a circular shadow?

In the third century B.C., a Greek named Eratosthenes figured out the distance around the Earth. He had been told that at the town of Syene (now called Aswan) in Egypt, the sun could be seen reflected from water in a deep well at noon on June 21. This meant the sun was directly overhead. At noon on the same day, Eratosthenes measured the angle of sunlight falling on Alexandria, a city at the mouth of the Nile River. He knew the distance from Alexandria to Syene. With these pieces of information, he calculated the distance around the Earth to be 24,500 miles. Today we know that the Earth's circumference —at the equator—is almost exactly 24,900 miles. (Around the poles, the distance is about 40 miles less.)

In 1810, an English scientist, Henry Cavendish, "weighed" the Earth. Of course, he had no scale to put the Earth on. Instead, he did an experiment based on the force of gravitation. He then made a calculation based on the experiment. He found that the Earth weighs 6,592 million million million tons. Scientists today, with the most modern equipment, find that Cavendish's answer was very accurate.

For further information on:

Earth's Composition, *see* GAS, HYDROGEN, METAL, MINERAL, NITROGEN, OXYGEN, WATER.

Earth's Features, *see* AFRICA, ANTARCTICA, ARCTIC, ASIA, CON-

EARTH HISTORY   Earth history is the study of the creation and formation of the Earth. Today, scientists think that the sun, the Earth, and the other planets in our solar system were formed at least five billion years ago. Many scientists believe that they were made from the shrinking and clumping together of a vast cloud of dust and gas in space. They think that the clump that formed the Earth was cold. The sun was cooler than it is today, but it was still very hot.

The Earth and its atmosphere formed a sphere hundreds of times larger than it is today. The atmosphere was tens of thousands of miles deep. Ninety-nine per cent of it was made up of the gases hydrogen and helium, the two lightest elements.

The huge sun-clump shrank, slowly at first, then faster and faster. As it became smaller, it heated up. It took about 80 million years to shrink to its present size. Toward the end of this time, the sun flared up, becoming brighter and hotter than it is today. During this flare up, which lasted several million years, the sun poured out tremendous amounts of heat and light.

THE MOLTEN EARTH. The Earth shrank and became warmer, too. Atomic reactions, called *radioactivity,* took place within the Earth. These produced large amounts of heat. As a result, the Earth melted. Heavy materials, such as iron, sank to the center. The lighter materials, those that eventually formed rocks, floated to the surface. The lightest of these probably clumped

▼*Volcanic activity was widespread during the early history of the Earth. But the surface of the Earth gradually cooled enough so that the oceans could form. (Pictures with this article by Charles R. Knight, © Field Museum of Natural History.)*

CHAPTERS IN EARTH'S HISTORY

This chart shows all the important changes that took place during the past history of the Earth. Beginning at the bottom of the chart, you can follow the history of the Earth all the way up to the present.

CENOZOIC ERA — The Age of Mammals. Lasted 60 million years to the present time.	QUATERNARY PERIOD	Recent Epoch Lasted 25,000 years.		Humans grew crops, herded animals, built cities, and kept written records. Early types of mammals died out. Climate became warmer when last glacier melted. Many mountains were rising.
		Pleistocene Epoch Lasted 1 million years.		Cave-dwelling, tool-making, fire-using humans spread throughout the earth. Lions, tigers, gorillas, and other modern animals appeared. Four glaciers, each followed by a warm period, caused migrations and the dying out of many animals. Mountains continued to rise.
	TERTIARY PERIOD	Pliocene Epoch Lasted 12 million years.		Man-like apes appeared. First hoofed horses appeared. Climate was cool. Sierra Nevada and Rocky Mountains rose, and the Alps, Caucasus, and Himalayas continued rising.
		Miocene Epoch Lasted 12 million years.		First bears and modern grazing animals appeared. Modern whales and other sea mammals appeared. The dog and cat families increased in number and size. Grasslands took the place of many forests. Climate was cool, and land was high and dry.
		Oligocene Epoch Lasted 10 million years.		Monkeys, apes, and meat-eating mammals appeared, along with squirrels, beavers, and other rodents. Mammals became gigantic in size. Giant hogs, as well as elephant- and rhinoceros-like mammals appeared. Climate was warm and wet. Land was low and moist.
		Eocene Epoch Lasted 20 million years.		Ancestors of the monkey and ape first appeared. Huge-toothed whales lived in the ocean. The ancestor of the horse—a cat-sized, four-toed animal—appeared. Palms and sequoia trees appeared. Climate was hot and rainy. Mountains were worn down by erosion.
		Paleocene Epoch Lasted 5 million years.		Small mammals were the main kind of land animal. Ancestors of rabbits, mice, squirrels, dogs, cats, and modern birds appeared. Climate was cool and dry. Mountains and other land areas were high.
ERA — Reptiles. years.		Cretaceous Period Lasted 65 million years.		Dinosaurs, flying reptiles, toothed birds, and other kinds of animals suddenly died out. Small mammals spread all over the Earth. Flowering plants appeared. Trees that lose leaves in cold weather spread worldwide. Climate was warm, and lands remained low.

MESOZOIC ... The Age of ... Lasted 155 m...

Triassic Period Lasted 45 million years.	Reptiles increased greatly in numbers and kinds. Amphibians decreased. Cone-bearing trees became the main kind of land plants. Climate suddenly became cold. The land rose higher than ever before, and many volcanoes erupted.

PALEOZOIC ERA — The Age of Trilobites, Fish, and Amphibians. Lasted 370 million years

Permian Period Lasted 50 million years.	Trilobites decreased in number. The first seed plants (cone-bearing trees) appeared. Climate got warmer when glaciers melted. Gas, oil, and salt were formed in the Earth.
Pennsylvanian Period Lasted 30 million years.	The first reptiles, snails, and seed plants appeared. Coal-forming forests grew thickly in swampy areas. Climate was mild, and oceans continued to flood the continents.
Mississippian Period Lasted 35 million years.	Amphibians were the main kind of animal. Giant insects appeared. Large, swampy areas were covered with forests of coal-forming trees. Climate was mild and warm. Lands remained low and were flooded by the oceans.
Devonian Period Lasted 60 million years.	Many armored fish and sharks lived in the ocean. Insects and the first spiders appeared. Amphibians became the first land animals. Climate was warm. The Appalachian and Ural Mountains were formed.
Silurian Period Lasted 20 million years.	The first air-breathing animals (probably similar to scorpions or lungfish) appeared. First land plants appeared. Oceans flooded the low lands. Climate was mild and becoming warmer.
Ordovician Period Lasted 75 million years.	Great numbers of trilobites existed, and starfish appeared. Fish with backbones and coral animals appeared. Climate was very warm.
Cambrian Period Lasted 100 million years.	Trilobites were the main kind of animal life. All animals lived in the oceans, and none had backbones. Shell-fish and snails appeared. Many forms of seaweed existed. Climate was cool at the beginning but became very warm by the middle of the period.

PRECAMBRIAN ERA

The Age of the Earliest Life Forms. Lasted 4 billion years.

In the early part of this period, the Earth's crust was becoming solid and volcanoes were erupting. No life existed during that time, but many rocks and minerals were being formed. Later in the period, bacteria grew and very simple life forms—amoebas, algae, worms, jellyfish—appeared in the ocean.

▲*Various forms of marine animal and plant life that lived 430 million years ago. Abundant land life had not yet developed.*

together in one large mass with an area equal to the area of all the continents today. The planet began to cool after a long time, and the outer 20 miles of the Earth formed a crust of solid rock. The melting and cooling took about a billion years.

As the Earth melted and then cooled, gases were given off. Some of these gases, mainly nitrogen and carbon dioxide, formed a new atmosphere. Much water vapor existed, too. The vapor formed an unbroken canopy of clouds, hundreds of miles thick, around the Earth. Violent lightning bolts hammered at the planet, and the rumble of thunder never ended. Although torrents of rain fell, the Earth remained dry. Any raindrops that reached the hot, rocky surface boiled upward in steam, rejoining the clouds from which they came.

THE OCEAN AND THE CONTINENTS. The Earth finally cooled enough so that rain could remain on its surface. Rainwater formed streams and rivers and ran to the low-lying areas. This water collected in pools, and the pools joined, eventually forming one huge ocean that covered nearly three-fourths of the planet. The only land that remained above water was made up of the lightest rock, which had floated highest on the surface when the Earth was molten.

As the ocean grew, the cloud canopy became thinner and thinner. It eventually broke up, and sunlight reached the Earth. Weather and seasons began. This happened more than four billion years ago.

Recording Earth's History

Man knows of his own history largely from written records. The Earth has kept records, too. Scientists have hunted for these records and learned to read Earth's "language," and each time a new discovery is made and translated, man learns a little more about the history of his planet.

Scientists have divided Earth's very long history into sections. The longest ones are called *eras*. At several times in Earth's history, widespread and rapid folding of Earth's crust has built huge mountain chains. Each time of mountain building is called a *revolution*. Each revolution marks the end of one era

▼*Land plants first formed in abundance on the Earth about 350 million years ago. They provided food and shelter for the growing number of animals that moved across the land.*

and the beginning of the next. Each era represents hundreds of millions of years.

Each era is divided into *periods*. The *Carboniferous* period, in which deposits of coal, oil, and natural gas were formed, lasted about 70 million years.

The most recent era, the Cenozoic, is still going on. Scientists have more information about this era than any other, so its periods have also been divided into *epochs*. All of these time periods together are referred to as *geologic time*, which is measured by changes in the Earth's surface.

Scientists use two kinds of records to make up these divisions. One is the rocks and soil and how they are arranged. The other is the *fossils*, the remains or traces of long-dead plants and animals. These records tell a fascinating story about the Earth. To relate every detail would take many books, but in the chart of Earth's history, you can see the major changes in the Earth.

For further information on:

Anthropology, *see* ANTHROPOLOGY, MAN, STONE AGE.

Astronomy, *see* ASTRONOMY, COMET, EARTH, MOON, SOLAR SYSTEM, SUN, UNIVERSE.

Atmosphere, *see* ATMOSPHERE, CLOUD, SKY, WEATHER.

Biology, *see* ALGAE; AMPHIBIAN; ANIMAL KINGDOM; BACTERIA; DARWIN, CHARLES; DINOSAUR; ECOLOGY; EVOLUTION; FOSSIL; LIFE; PLANT KINGDOM; PROTIST; REPTILE.

Chemistry and Physics, *see* ELEMENT, GAS, HYDROGEN, NITROGEN, OXYGEN, RADIATION, RADIOACTIVITY.

Earth, *see* CONTINENT, EROSION, MINERAL, OCEAN, SOIL.

Geology, *see* CANYON, EARTHQUAKE, GEOLOGY, GLACIER, ICE AGE, RIVER, VOLCANO.

EARTHQUAKE The people of Charleston, South Carolina, felt the ground shake several times on August 31, 1886. Each tremor was a little stronger than the one before. A rumbling sound seemed to approach the city. The rumble increased to a roar, as if a huge train were rushing through a tunnel under the town. The ground rose and fell in waves. All these events lasted a little more than a minute. Eight minutes later the ground shook and rumbled again.

▲ *Some of the animals that roamed the wild terrain of California 100,000 years ago: wolf (left), saber-toothed cat (right), horses of a species long extinct (rear), and a group of huge birds.*

EARTHWORM

▲*An earthquake struck Anchorage, a city in Alaska, in March, 1964. Property damage totaled hundreds of millions of dollars, and 130 persons died. The quake also generated a huge tidal wave, or* tsunami, *which was felt as far away as California.*

The most destructive of U.S. earthquakes were in San Francisco in 1906 (about 700 people killed, 500 million dollars in damages), and in Alaska in 1964 (130 killed, over 500 million dollars in damages).

People were thrown off their feet by the shaking of the earth. Chimneys and walls fell into crumbled heaps of rubbish. Every building in Charleston was damaged. Many persons were injured or killed by falling buildings. Cracks, called *fissures,* opened in the ground. Railway tracks were twisted.

The shaking of the earth was an *earthquake,* a sudden violent movement of part of the Earth's crust. The sudden movement is caused by the breaking of rocks that are under great pressure. The pressure comes from forces deep inside the earth—sometimes from 100 to more than 450 miles deep—that build mountains by bending the planet's rocky crust. Pressure on one or more layers of rock goes on for many years, becoming stronger as time passes. The pressure finally becomes more than the rock can withstand. The rock breaks and snaps back, shaking the earth for miles around.

The tremors caused by earthquakes are recorded and measured with a seismograph. A seismograph often consists of a large weight that hangs from a framework resting on a fixed base in the earth (rock). When an earthquake causes tremors in the earth, the base of the seismograph moves. But the weight remains still. The amount of movement the base makes is recorded and traced on a chart. This chart, or seismogram, provides a record of the earth's movement.

Not all earthquakes cause damage or injury. Most are so mild that the trembling of the earth is noticed only by persons at rest. About 150,000 earthquakes occur each year, but only about 100 are very destructive.

Sometimes earthquakes under the ocean cause landslides. These landslides can cause very large waves, called seismic sea waves. They are often incorrectly called tidal waves.

No part of the Earth is entirely free of earthquakes, but in most regions earthquakes are faint. New England, for example, has had only one strong earthquake in thousands of years, but it has many small ones yearly. If you mark on a world map the places where earthquakes often occur, your marks will form two large belts—the Pacific belt and the Mediterranean belt. If you also mark on this map the places where new mountains are slowly rising, these marks will be within the earthquake belts, since the forces that build mountains also cause earthquakes.

ALSO READ: EARTH, EARTH HISTORY, GEOLOGY, MOUNTAIN.

EARTHWORM Earthworms are very popular as bait for fishing, or angling. Another name for them is "angleworms." They are usually easy to find in moist garden soil or around lawns. Their reddish-brown bodies are made up of many ring-like parts, or *segments.* Little bristles attached to the segments help the worms move through the earth. An earthworm is damp and clammy to the touch. This is because its body has a

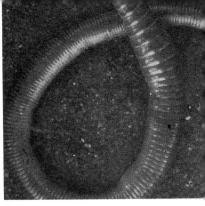

slimy coating to keep it from drying out. The pointed end that looks like a tail is really its head. If the first few segments of the worm's head are cut off, new head segments grow back. The earthworm can also grow back a new tail if its tail is cut off.

Earthworms eat bits of leaves, grass, and decayed plant matter in the earth. They come to the surface of the ground at night to feed. They also mate at night. The worm lays its eggs in a cocoon after mating. This cocoon is produced by the worm's body. The young worms that hatch from the cocoon are small but fully developed.

Earthworms are very helpful to farmers and gardeners. They help keep the soil good for growing plants. One way they do this is by hollowing out many little tunnels underground. This keeps the soil loose, making spaces for air and rainwater to seep into the soil. Earthworms also turn the soil over and break it up by eating it. As an earthworm tunnels, it eats the soil that is in its path. The soil is finely ground up in the worm's digestive system. Only the plant matter in the soil is digested.

Earthworms usually stay underground by day, but if a hard rain floods their burrows, they come up to the surface. Just after a rainstorm is a good time to hunt for earthworms. If you want to keep one to watch for a while, put it in a box with plenty of damp soil. Remember, it must burrow. Do not leave it in the sun or on a radiator, because strong light can kill it. Put leaves and grass on the soil.

ALSO READ: ANIMAL KINGDOM, WORM.

▲ *The body of the common earthworm is made up of about 150 segments.*

EASTER   Easter is a day of great joy for Christians. They believe that on the first Easter Jesus arose from the dead.

Easter is always celebrated on a Sunday in early spring. But it comes on a different date each year. This is because it always takes place on the first Sunday after the first full moon after the spring equinox (March 21). So Easter can come anytime from March 22 to April 25.

The week before Easter is called *Holy Week.* It begins with *Palm Sunday,* which celebrates the day Jesus rode into Jerusalem and the people scattered palm leaves before him. Christ's Last Supper is celebrated on *Maundy* or *Holy Thursday.* His death on the cross is commemorated on *Good Friday.*

On Easter Sunday, people dress up in new spring clothes and go to church. Many churches have special sunrise services. Easter baskets are given on this day. They contain candy and colorful decorated eggs. Eggs are associated with Easter because they are a symbol of new life. Children are often told that Easter eggs are brought and hidden by the Easter Bunny. This legend probably comes from an old German folk tale.

ALSO READ: CARNIVAL, CHRISTIANITY, JESUS CHRIST.

EAST GERMANY see GERMANY.

▼ *An old Easter card with the greetings for the holiday and an egg as the symbol of new life.*

EAST INDIA COMPANY   Portugal was the first nation to trade in India and the Far East. Portuguese explorers first came to India in 1498. Other European countries wanted a share of the wealth in spices, silks, porcelain, and other goods found in these faraway lands. The British, French, Dutch, and other nationalities established private trading organizations, each called the East India Company.

The British East India Company, founded in 1600, became the most powerful and the longest lasting of the trading companies. It was in operation for more than 250 years. The French East India Company tried to push the British out of India, but they failed. By the 1800s, the British company controlled most of the Indian trade—and also ruled most of India! In 1857, Indian soldiers working for the British company rebelled in what is called the Sepoy Rebellion. The Indians were defeated. But afterwards, the British government took the control of India away from the British East India Company.

The Dutch East India Company was also quite powerful. It traded for spices in the islands of the East Indies. In 1798, the Dutch government took control of the lands that this company had ruled.

ALSO READ: INDIA, TRADE.

ECHIDNA see SPINY ANTEATER

ECHINODERM   Echinoderms are small invertebrates (animals without backbones) that live on the bottom of the sea. The best-known echinoderms are starfish. Other common echinoderms are sea urchins, sea cucumbers, brittle stars, sand dollars, and sea lilies.

The word "echinoderm" means "spiny-skinned." Most of the animals called echinoderms have many small spines—or stiff little points—growing from their skin. If you look at a starfish, you can see that its main body is in the center and that it has five arms that stick out like a five-pointed star. Other echinoderms also have body parts grouped around a center part, although the pattern is not always easy to see from the outside.

Major Echinoderms

STARFISH. Starfish live on the bottom of the sea in bays and shallow water. Some are as big around as a 25-cent coin. Others are three feet across. Most starfish have five arms, although some have seven arms or more. If a starfish loses an arm, it can grow another arm to take its place. If some kinds of starfish are cut into pieces, a new starfish will grow from each arm.

A starfish creeps along the bottom of the sea in a peculiar way. It has many hollow, tube-like feet on the underside of its arms. To take a step, the starfish lets water into the tube feet of one of its arms. The water makes the arm stretch out. Suckers

▼Starfish have very poor eyesight. Tiny eyespots, located on the tip of each arm, sense light but cannot perceive objects. The round, spiny sea urchin is a relative of the starfish.

on the ends of the tube feet hold on to rocks on the sea bottom. That is one step. The starfish then lets water into the tube feet of another arm. The second arm stretches out, and the starfish takes another step. The starfish moves each of its five arms in turn. It can move pretty fast when it has to.

A starfish also eats in a peculiar way. A starfish's mouth is under its body. It eats by moving on top of its food, opening its mouth, and then letting its stomach come out of its mouth until the stomach covers the food and digests it. Starfish especially like to eat clams and oysters. The soft inside of each clam or oyster is protected by two hard shells. To get at an oyster, the starfish covers the shells with its arms. The suckers on the bottom of the arms hold tight to the shells of the oyster. The starfish then pulls the oyster shells apart with its very powerful arms.

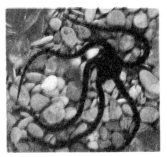
▲ *A brittle star.*

BRITTLE STAR. Brittle stars live at the bottom of the ocean where the water is very deep and cold. A brittle star looks more like a spider than a starfish. It has very long, thin arms, with which it can move very fast. If one of the arms breaks off, another arm grows in its place.

SEA URCHIN. Sea urchins look like round balls covered with long, sharp spines that look something like the quills on a porcupine. The spines protect the sea urchin against its enemies. Some kinds of sea urchins have poison in the tips of their spines. So if you see a sea urchin, be careful not to touch it.

SEA CUCUMBER. A sea cucumber has a sausage-shaped body and a cluster of sticky tentacles, or feelers, surrounding its mouth. The sea cucumber is a sluggish creature. It usually waits for its food to come to it. It catches tiny sea animals with its tentacles. The Chinese like to eat dried sea cucumber, which they call *trepang*.

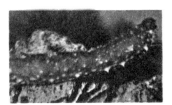
▲ *A sea cucumber.*

ALSO READ: ANIMAL DEFENSES, ANIMAL KINGDOM, NATURE STUDY, OCEAN.

ECHO see SOUND.

ECLIPSE Nearly 2,600 years ago, warring soldiers from ancient countries of Media and Lydia faced each other across an open plain. Both sides expected victory. But the soldiers from Lydia had a secret weapon. The weapon was a prediction from an astronomer named Thales. Thales predicted that the sun would darken that day.

The battle began. Soldiers fought bravely for hours. Both armies were strong, and neither army was winning. A black shadow suddenly crawled across the sun. Soldiers from Lydia cried out with joy and attacked harder. But the soldiers from Media felt great fear. Why did the sun turn black? What great power brought darkness in the middle of the day? The Media warriors dropped their weapons and ran away, and the battle

▲ *A solar eclipse caused by the moon. The corona, a shimmering halo of light, brightens the darkened sky as the moon passes between the Earth and the sun.*

ended. Lydia won because Thales predicted a solar eclipse and warned the soldiers.

A *solar eclipse* happens when the moon moves directly between the Earth and the sun. The moon blocks out light from the sun for a short time. The moon's shadow falls on Earth. As the moon moves in its orbit, the shadow moves across the Earth. The shadow is small, so only a small part of Earth sees it.

Does it seem strange to you that one object can appear to block out another, much larger object? Look out a window at something about a block away—for example, a car or a traffic light. Hold a dime at arm's length between the object and you, and close one eye. You can still see the object around the edges of the dime. Bring the dime close to your eye and look again. This time, you can see the dime but not the object behind it. An eclipse works on the same principle.

The center of the shadow is a dark circle called the *umbra*. It is only about 167 miles across. Inside the umbra, the eclipse is complete—the moon completely hides the sun. Around the umbra is a 2,000-mile-wide circle of less shadow. This dense circle is the *penumbra*. Inside the penumbra, the eclipse is not seen as complete. Part of the sun is still visible. Solar eclipses do not last very long. They are over in a few minutes.

Never look at a solar eclipse. The sun's rays are so bright—even during an eclipse—that you can be blinded. The brightness makes it very difficult to see what happens, anyway. Instead, watch the eclipse on television. Special equipment, including telescopes and filters, makes it much easier to see the eclipse. And an expert astronomer will explain exactly what is happening.

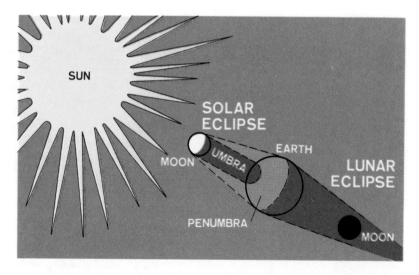

A *lunar eclipse* happens when the Earth moves between the sun and the moon. The Earth's shadow stops all sunlight from reaching the moon. Lunar eclipses are visible only at night. The Earth's shadow starts at one edge of the moon. The entire moon is soon covered by the shadow. It cannot be seen at all.

A lunar eclipse lasts several hours, because the Earth's shadow is so big. The moon finally moves out of the shadow and reappears in the sky. Partial eclipses also happen when the moon moves through an edge of the shadow instead of going through the middle.

ALSO READ: ASTRONOMY, MOON, SUN.

As many as seven or as few as two eclipses happen each year. If there are seven, either four or five will be solar. If there are two, both will be solar.

ECOLOGY Several years ago, a boy lived near a lake where he often fished and swam. He became interested in the life of the lake, and he began to study the lake and the nearby meadows and woods.

The boy soon learned that bass, perch, and pickerel swam in the lake and that many kinds of plants, including reeds and water lilies, grew in the water. The boy looked more carefully and found large numbers of minnows and other tiny fishes. With a microscope, the boy found many kinds of even smaller living things in the water, including amoebas and hydras.

The boy also noticed that birds, squirrels, and mice came to the lake to drink. So did cows. The boy's dog often took a drink from the lake. And once, while the boy sat quietly behind a bush, a thirsty deer paid a visit. The squirrels and birds made their homes in the woods. So did many other animals, such as foxes and rabbits. One day the boy found a blacksnake, which he knew was harmless. He had read that blacksnakes eat field mice, pests that eat farmers' grain. The boy found mice living in the meadow—he had guessed that they would be there after he found the snake. He also discovered many insects, including grasshoppers and butterflies.

The longer the boy watched the lake, woods, and meadow, the more he realized how all the *organisms* (living things) that made their homes there depended on each other. The areas of the lake, the meadow, and the woods are called *habitats*. Habitats are areas where certain organisms usually live. The snake could not have lived in the meadow habitat if no mice were nearby. The mice needed grain and seeds from farms and gardens. The deer needed the woods and the clear, cool lake water. So did many birds and other animals. And the fish, too, depended on the lake. If the lake dried up or if its water became salty, the fish would all die.

One summer, very little rain fell. There were almost no mosquitoes that year, and the boy was glad. But then he realized that there were fewer fish because the fish's supply of food—which included mosquitoes—was smaller than usual.

The boy realized that all the creatures of the lake, woods, and meadow lived together in a *community,* just as the people of a town form a community. No living thing can exist alone. Every living thing is surrounded by air, water, or soil. And every living

▼ *Algae, flowers, frogs, lily pads, trees, and many other forms of life make up the ecology of a swamp.*

thing takes things from its surroundings—its *environment*—and leaves other things.

The boy may not have known it, but he was doing an *ecological* study. Ecology is the science that studies how all living things depend on each other and on their environment. Environments include the boy's lake, meadow, and woods. Many things help make up an environment—climate, atmosphere, soil, land shape, height above sea level, the kinds of plants that grow, even the number of people that visit and what the people do. Animals and plants survive in environments that are suited to them. Palm trees do not grow in the Arctic, where it is cold. They do not grow in every warm place, either, but only where the right soil and water conditions exist. Birds that nest in trees do not live on grassy plains or high up on mountains, where no trees grow.

The boy's lake, woods, and forest and all the organisms in them make up an *ecosystem*—all the organisms of a community, plus all the surrounding things that are not living and never were alive.

Ways Living Things Interact

Living things depend on one another in many ways. Lions are predators—they kill other animals for food. Man is a predator, too, since he kills animals for food.

A relationship with similar effects exists between parasites and their hosts. A *parasite* is a living thing that lives in or on another living thing (its *host*) and that takes food directly from its host. Smut, a fungus that lives on corn, is a parasite. So are blood-sucking ticks and fleas. Tapeworms are parasites that attach themselves to the intestines of human beings. A parasite usually does not kill its host, but it may make the host weak.

Another kind of relationship between living things is *commensalism,* which comes from Latin words meaning "eating at the same table." You can see how this type of relationship was named by studying two fishes, the remora and the shark. The remora is a small fish with a kind of suction cup on its head. The remora uses this cup to attach itself to a shark. This has no effect on the shark, but it is good for the remora in two ways. First, the remora gets a free ride (the shark is a faster, stronger swimmer). Second, scraps from the shark's dinner float by the remora, which quickly gobbles them up. A commensal relationship is good for one living thing and has no effect on the other.

Another kind of relationship is called *mutualism* (from the Latin word for "trade" or "exchange"). Squirrels, chipmunks, and other animals that store acorns for winter food share a mutualistic relationship with oak trees. These trees provide food for the animals. A few of the acorns that the animals bury are not found. These acorns sprout, and new oak trees grow.

Animals may also be involved in *competition.* This may occur between two plants or animals of the same species (kind). Two frogs, for example, cannot catch and eat the same insect—one frog must trap another insect or go hungry. Two maple trees cannot grow in the same square foot of ground. The stronger tree survives; the other dies.

Competition also goes on between species. Green plants cannot live without sunlight. In thick forests, trees block all sunlight, so that none reaches the forest floor. Grass and flowers cannot grow on such a forest floor. Another example of competition exists between bluebirds and starlings. Bluebirds nest in empty woodpecker holes. So do starlings, and in areas where both bluebirds and starlings live, they must compete for available space.

▲*Waste products from factories damage lakes, rivers, and streams. In some areas waterways have become so polluted that plants and animals needed in the food web have been killed.*

The Food Web

People sometimes think about how their food comes to them. Have you ever thought about how the fish you eat for dinner got to your table? The story probably starts with green algae, tiny one-celled organisms that are eaten by very small fish. The fish are eaten by bigger fish, which are eaten by even bigger fish, until finally a big fish is caught for a tasty meal.

But the way in which living things feed on each other is not really so simple. If you trace a spider web with your finger, you will find that, sooner or later, you return to the spot you started from. It is that way with food, too.

You probably already know that green plants use the sun's energy to produce food from substances in the soil, and that all animals depend on green plants for food. For example, in the boy's meadow and woods that you read about, rabbits, mice, and grasshoppers (and other animals, too) eat the plants. Snakes and foxes then eat these animals. And if a hawk gliding overhead spots a fat blacksnake, then the hawk may get a meal, too. (If there were no green plants for the rabbits, mice, and grasshoppers to feed on, what would the snakes and foxes eat? If there were no green plants for cattle to feed on, what would you eat?)

This part of the *food web* sounds like the fish dinner you just read about. But spider webs and food webs lead in several directions, and the next part of the food web leads back to the beginning, green plants. A farmer or gardener sometimes gives his plants fertilizer to make sure they get all the substances they need for growth. Who provides fertilizer for wild plants? Animals and other plants do. Animals all produce waste. And all animals and plants die. Bacteria that live in soil *decompose* (break down) the bodies of dead organisms and the waste products of living organisms. Bacteria return necessary chemicals to the soil, growing plants use the chemicals, and the food web goes

▲*Planting trees is a good way to use idle land and improve the quality of the environment. What can you do to improve the environment in your neighborhood?*

▼*These old newspapers will be carried to a* recycling *plant. They will be churned back into paper and re-sold, perhaps to be made into newspapers again. Burning trash causes waste and fouls the air. Recycling trash saves trees, keeps the air clean, and helps eliminate garbage dumps.*

on. Can you see how other plants and animals might fit in? Where would a mosquito fit? What about a man? What about the insect-eating plant called Venus's-flytrap? This food web is just one example of the *balance of nature.* Each part of nature needs every other part in order to exist. If one part of nature dies out or becomes too strong, every other part of nature is eventually affected by the change.

Studying ecology can be expensive and complicated. Some ecologists need helicopters or deep-sea diving equipment. But studying ecology can also be easy and fun. Pick a small land area near your home, perhaps a back yard or park. Is the land flat or hilly? Does the ground get a lot of sun, or just a little? Is there grass? Are there many rocks? Are there trees? How many? How many kinds? Does the soil usually feel damp or dry? Study your land for a year. Is there snow? Do the trees lose their leaves? What animals live on your land at least part of the time? What do they eat? Look in tree bark and under rocks. Dig in the ground, if that is allowed. Do you find insects, spiders, centipedes, or other "bugs"? Can you find seeds? Can you find any decomposing matter? How many lives are going on in your area? Can you trace the food web?

What Makes Ecology Important?

When you are sick, you go to a doctor—the person who knows what is wrong with you and what you must do to be healthy again. Ecologists are "doctors" for the environment. They can tell what has made the environment sick and what can make it better. The world has been in constant change since it was formed. Not all changes are harmful. For example, your body is changing all the time. Your heart beats faster when you run than it does when you sleep. If your heartbeat did not change, you would probably collapse every time you ran.

Changes in the environment are not all bad, but man's inventions and discoveries are causing rapid changes in some ways that are not healthy. The air is being filled with poisons. Waterways that were once clean and filled with living things are becoming sewers where almost nothing can live. Man must learn to *adapt* himself to his environment. *Adaptation* means changing or adjusting in order to fit in with the environment or surroundings. Man will go on making inventions and discoveries. Ecologists can help all people understand the ways in which all living things fit together. And they can help find ways to use the inventions and discoveries without making the world sick.

For further information on:

Animal and Plant Life, *see* AGRICULTURE, ALGAE, ANIMAL DEFENSES, ANIMAL DISTRIBUTION, ANIMAL HOMES, ARCTIC LIFE, BIRDS OF THE PAST, CITY WILDLIFE, DESERT, FOOD WEB, HIBERNATION, JUNGLE, MARINE LIFE, PARASITE, PLANT

DISTRIBUTION, POND LIFE, PRAIRIE, RARE ANIMALS, SWAMPS AND MARSHES, TUNDRA.

Conservation, *see* CONSERVATION, COMMUNITY, EROSION, FOREST FIRE, LUMBER AND LUMBERING, NATIONAL PARK, NATURAL RESOURCES, PARK, SOIL, WATER SUPPLY, WILDERNESS AREA.

ECONOMICS Can you buy everything you want with your allowance? Probably you have to choose what you can *afford* to buy out of all the things you *want* to buy. If you decide that you want or need many things, you must figure out how to earn or save the money to pay for them. Just as you have to make these decisions with the money you earn or receive as an allowance, your parents must figure out how they can buy the things your family wants and needs. (Cars, television sets—even food—can be very expensive.)

A nation has the same problem. Its people want many things, such as food, clothes, houses, cars, and furniture. Each nation must find a way to make or buy as many of these things as possible and find a way to distribute and sell them to people. The field of *economics* studies the way a nation handles the problems of making, distributing, and buying all the various things that its people want and need.

What is Economics?

Economics is a social science that is affected by three basic things—natural resources, labor, and capital. *Natural resources* are things on or in the Earth, such as water, trees, and ores. *Labor* is the effort of people who work to turn natural resources into products or who perform services. The word *capital* can mean one of two things. Capital can be the money needed to build factories and stores and to buy machines and tools. Capital can also be anything made or produced by people that is used to produce something else. The machines and tools themselves are examples of capital.

Three of the processes studied by economists are production, distribution, and exchange. A factory that makes furniture is engaged in *production*. The furniture is usually sold to a wholesale company that in turn sells it to many different retail stores. The furniture has to be delivered from the factory to the wholesale company, and from there it goes to the retail stores. In the retail stores, salesmen will sell it to people who want furniture. The delivering and selling is called *distribution.*

At each step, a number of people must be paid for their work in getting the furniture to the customers who finally buy it. This means that some money goes to the factory workers who made the furniture, some to the workers who loaded it onto trucks, some to the truck drivers, some to warehouse workers, some to the wholesale companies that sell it to the retail stores, some to the retail stores, and some to the clerks who sell it to the customers. Since money is exchanged in all these steps, the process is called *exchange*.

After everyone is paid for his work in the furniture industry, as in all industries, there should be money left over. This money is *profit*. Everyone involved in the process of making, delivering, and selling the furniture expects to make a profit. But perhaps the factories or the stores do not sell all their furniture. Maybe the supply of furniture was greater than the demand for (or desire to buy) furniture. Or perhaps the price they asked for the furniture was too low to pay everyone for their work. Then they have had a *loss*. They have less money in the bank. Or perhaps they have to borrow money or even sell their factory.

Production, distribution, and exchange are affected by many other things besides salaries and profit. For example, the U.S. must buy such goods as coffee, tea, and sugar from other countries. Other countries in turn buy wheat, steel, and other goods from the U.S. This *international trade* affects shipping, banking, communications, marketing, and other services.

International trade is an extension of domestic trade and domestic *competition*. In competition, nations and business rivals—such as those in the automobile industry—try to outdo each other. Car makers offer all sorts of deals to car buyers. They compete with each other in order to get more business —and more profit—than their rivals. Some U.S. companies make small cars to compete with small cars that are imported from foreign countries. Prices could be very high without competition. If only one company made all automobiles, a buyer would have no choice of prices. Such a company would have a *monopoly*, which is illegal in the United States. But in a private enterprise system (called *capitalism*), a policy of *laissez faire,* or non-interference, is important. In a *laissez faire* system, a government does not try to control trade or interfere with competition unless it becomes absolutely necessary.

Many other factors are involved in economics. Some goods may be hard to get. When there is more money available than usual, prices tend to rise, because people can afford to pay the higher costs. This is called *inflation*. Poor management, demand for goods, strikes by workers—all of these factors and more affect the daily lives of people in some way.

Socialism

Another kind of economic system is *socialism*. Under socialism, a government owns and manages most big industries—including electric power, gas, coal, transportation, and communications. These industries are all run so that everyone shares their benefits. Profit from large industries does not go to private individuals. Small businesses and private homes are still owned by individuals. England, Sweden, and Israel, among other countries, have adopted the system of socialism.

Communism

A third system, *Communism,* seeks to do away with all ownership of property by individuals. Not only factories and large industries, but even homes and farms are owned by the government for the benefit of all the people. Under ideal Communism, all people share goods according to what they need.

Whether a nation's economic system is capitalist, socialist, or Communist, all economic systems are based on the fact that people must have food, clothing, and housing. There must be workers to produce, distribute, and sell the goods, and consumers to buy and use the goods. Therefore, workers and consumers form the basis of economics.

For further information on:

Business Management and Organization, *see* ADVERTISING, CORPORATION, STORES AND SHOPS.

Economic Systems, *see* CAPITALISM, COMMUNISM, SOCIALISM.

Factors of Production, *see* AGRICULTURE, AUTOMATION, MANUFACTURING, NATURAL RESOURCES, PUBLIC UTILITY, SUPPLY AND DEMAND.

Finance, *see* ACCOUNTING AND BOOKKEEPING, BANKS AND BANKING, INSURANCE, STOCKS AND BONDS, TAX.

History, *see* CHILD LABOR; DEPRESSION; FEUDALISM; INDUSTRIAL REVOLUTION; MARX, KARL.

International Economics, *see* COMMON MARKET, INTERNATIONAL TRADE, TRADE.

▼*A narrow street in Ambato, a town in central Ecuador. The men are wearing* ponchos, *warm blanket-like cloaks that fit easily over the head.*

ECUADOR   The small country of Ecuador lies on the Pacific coast of South America. To its north is Colombia, and to its south and east is Peru. Ecuador is about the same size as Oregon, but has three times as many people. Most of them are Indian or part Indian, and many speak only the Quechua language. About 10 per cent of the people are Europeans, and about 10 per cent are Negro or part Negro. Many people in Ecuador are very poor—especially the Indians, who still live in very primitive conditions.

The equator crosses the country. *Ecuador* is the Spanish word for equator. Two ranges of the Andes Mountains form a broad highland zone running north to south through Ecuador, separating it into three regions. (See the map with the article on SOUTH AMERICA.)

The humid coastal lowlands are the richest agricultural area. Here coffee, bananas, cacao, and rice are grown for export. Ecuador's largest city and chief port, Guayaquil, is found there.

More than half the people live in the cool high valleys of the

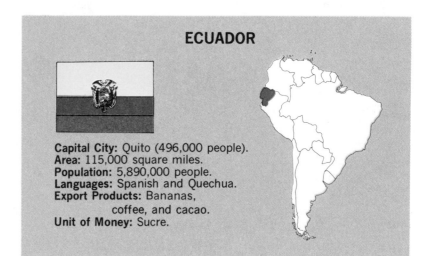

ECUADOR

Capital City: Quito (496,000 people).
Area: 115,000 square miles.
Population: 5,890,000 people.
Languages: Spanish and Quechua.
Export Products: Bananas,
           coffee, and cacao.
Unit of Money: Sucre.

central highlands. They raise cattle, sheep, and llamas. Grain, potatoes, fruits, and vegetables are grown in valleys surrounded by some of the highest volcanoes in South America. Ecuador's capital city, Quito, is in the highlands. Quito is a beautiful city with many buildings from the Spanish colonial period. Although Quito is near the equator, the climate is spring-like all year round because the city is 9,250 feet above sea level.

The hot, low plains east of the Andes are mostly tropical jungle where few people live. Rich oil deposits have recently been discovered which may help develop this area. In the deep forests live primitive Indians, including the Jivaros, who were once head-hunters.

Ecuador was part of an ancient Indian kingdom when the Inca Indians conquered it in about 1470. Francisco Pizarro led the Spanish expedition that overthrew the Inca Empire in 1533. A Venezuelan general, Antonio José de Sucre, helped Ecuador win freedom from Spain in 1822. Ecuador became a republic in 1830.

The Galapagos Islands, lying 600 miles off the Pacific Coast of South America, belong to Ecuador. They are famous for the giant land turtles and other animals found there.

ALSO READ: DARWIN, CHARLES; GALAPAGOS ISLANDS; INCA; PIZARRO, FRANCISCO; SOUTH AMERICA.

EDISON, THOMAS ALVA (1847-1931) What would we do without electric light bulbs, phonographs, motion picture cameras—things we take for granted? They were all invented by one man, Thomas Alva Edison. This great American inventor produced more than 1,000 inventions. Few men have had such a direct effect on the lives of people everywhere.

Edison was born in Milan, Ohio. He spent only three months in school. His teachers could not understand why he questioned everything he was told, so his mother decided to educate him herself. He soon developed a keen interest in science. Edison took a job as a newsboy on a train when he was 12. He bought a small printing press and printed a weekly newspaper in a baggage car. When he was 16, he became a telegraph operator and began to experiment with electrical instruments. His first major invention was an improved version of the stock ticker, a machine used by stockbrokers to record the purchase and sale of stocks.

Edison set up a laboratory at Menlo Park, New Jersey, in 1876. He improved the telephone so that it could carry a voice over a long distance. He invented the phonograph and developed one of the first motion picture cameras. Edison's greatest experiments were with electric light. A type of electric bulb, called an *arc light*, was already in use. But it was so bright that it could not be used indoors. Edison invented an *incandescent* light bulb, which contains a special wire, or filament. When electricity heats the filament, light is given off. The light bulbs used in homes today are similar to Edison's original bulb. By 1887, the inventor outgrew his laboratory in Menlo Park, and he moved to another one in West Orange, New Jersey.

Edison worked with amazing concentration. He always made sure that his inventions would be workable and useful. He often lived in his laboratory, taking only a few hours of sleep. By the end of his life, "The Wizard of Menlo Park" had been honored by countries all over the world.

ALSO READ: ELECTRICITY, INVENTION, LIGHTING, PHONOGRAPH, RECORDING, TELEPHONE.

EDUCATION   Think of all the things you learned how to do before you went to school! Education is not just going to school. It is the lifelong learning that takes place within a person as he deals with experiences of all kinds, makes decisions, forms opinions, and develops relationships with others. Everyone receives some kind of education just by learning from the experiences of life. *Schooling,* or the learning that takes place in a series of schools over a period of years, is usually called "formal education."

There was no formal education at all in very ancient times. Education was centered around the home. A boy simply learned to do exactly the same work as his father. He learned by watching his father and the other men in the tribe and by helping them. A girl learned all necessary skills she would need as an adult from her mother and the other women in the family or tribe. The children learned only the tasks needed for providing food, clothing, and shelter.

Methods for writing were first invented in ancient Sumer, Egypt, and Babylonia. Schools were founded to teach boys how to become scribes. Egyptian students learned to copy passages

▲*Thomas A. Edison making a recording on a phonograph, a machine which he invented in 1877.*

Henry Ford moved Edison's laboratory from Menlo Park, New Jersey, to Dearborn, Michigan, where people can visit it today. The inventor's laboratory and home in West Orange, New Jersey, are part of a national monument called the Edison National Historic Site.

▲ *Students examine the effects of bleach on various fabrics. Learning by doing makes education more fun and more meaningful than just hearing facts repeated.*

from literature on paper called papyrus. Their teachers often beat them to make them behave. The Egyptians had a saying, "A boy's ears are on his back; he hears when he is beaten." Boys in Babylonia learned to write by pressing a wedge-shaped stick into a wet clay tablet. The tablets dried and hardened. Many tablets have been found with this form of writing, called *cuneiform.* Both Egyptian and Babylonian priests gave more advanced training in professions such as medicine, architecture, or the priesthood. All education was practical. Boys were taught only what they needed to know for a specific profession.

Greek and Roman Schools

The ancient Greeks developed a broader idea of education. In Athens, for example, all adult men who were not slaves had to be able both to defend the city in wartime and to take part in its government. The Athenians believed that the best way to produce good citizens was to educate boys so that they developed many talents—not just the particular skills they needed for a single profession.

Boys in Athens started to school at the age of seven. Their classes were divided between gymnastics and music. The term "music" included reading, writing, and the study of literature. The boys copied poems and quotations from Greek literature on wax tablets with pointed sticks. They then read what they had copied and the teacher, who was sometimes a slave, explained it to them. They also learned to play musical instruments called *lyres* and to sing. They often did dances to express in movement the meaning of a poem. Gymnastics included running, jumping, wrestling, and throwing the discus (a circular plate of stone or metal) and the javelin (a spear). The boys also did calisthenics and played ball. The Athenians believed that every citizen should have "a sound mind in a sound body."

Mothers and fathers in early Rome had complete responsibility for educating their children. But government-controlled grammar schools were later established throughout the Roman Empire. These schools taught Greek and Latin. More advanced schools specialized in *rhetoric,* the art of public speaking.

The Middle Ages

The only European schools for several centuries after the fall of the Roman Empire were run by the Christian church. Their chief purpose was religious training.

Young men of noble families were trained to become knights. They started as *pages* at the castle of a noble. Pages waited on the lord and lady of the castle and were taught military skills and sometimes how to read and write. A page became a *squire* when he was 14 or 15. He assisted his lord in combat and waited on him. The squire was knighted at the age of 21.

◄Education takes place outside, as well as inside, the classroom. These children are enjoying a picnic lunch during a field trip.

The first European universities were founded toward the end of the Middle Ages. They were church schools established for the education of priests. They taught grammar, rhetoric, logic, music, arithmetic, geometry, and astronomy. Advanced degrees were given in medicine, law, and religious studies.

Craft education was controlled by the guilds in the town. A guild was an organization of workers in a particular craft, such as weaving, woodcarving, or shoemaking. A boy learned his trade by becoming an *apprentice* to a master craftsman. He worked in the master's shop in exchange for training in the craft. The master also provided the apprentice with clothes, food, and a place to sleep. When he was older, the apprentice became a *journeyman* and worked for daily wages. He might later become a master himself.

The Renaissance and the Reformation

The Renaissance was a period of "rebirth" of learning. It began in Italy in the fourteenth century and then spread to other parts of Europe. The Renaissance was marked by a new interest in the arts, literature, and culture of Greece and Rome. Renaissance educators adopted the Greek ideal of a well-rounded education. They were especially interested in the scientific study of man and the world of nature. This was very different from education during the Middle Ages, which had emphasized the study of religious ideas.

The Reformation followed the Renaissance. This was the period in which the Protestant churches were founded. The Protestants believed that everyone should be able to read the Bible. They were in favor of a basic education for everyone. They founded many new schools and reorganized many old ones. The Roman Catholic Church also began to make education available to more people at this time.

▲In the early 1800s, schools were small. They had few books and little equipment. Even so, a child was very lucky to go to such a school.

Free Public Schools

The Protestant reformer Martin Luther recommended that there be free public schools for everyone. But it was not until the 1800s that this started to become a common practice. The United States was a leader in public education. Many schools had only one room, in which students of all grades were taught. Americans believed that equal opportunity for all was possible only through a free public school system. Co-education (education of boys and girls together) in public schools also became widespread in the nineteenth century. By the time of the Civil War, most states had public elementary schools, and several hundred public high schools had been built. Many states also founded state universities. These schools charge low tuition (fees) to residents of the state.

Modern American Education

Today all children in the United States must go to school until they are at least 16. More than 50 million students attend public and private elementary schools, junior high schools, and high schools. Schools organize programs to help each student develop his special talents. Courses are offered in physical education, art, drama, literature, and music, as well as languages, sciences, and social studies. Courses in industrial arts and business skills prepare students who want to go into those fields when they finish high school.

Colleges and universities offer more advanced academic courses as well as training for professions such as medicine, law, engineering, teaching, or architecture. Many states have special agricultural colleges. Technical schools offer training beyond the high school level in such skills as mechanics, drafting, cabinetmaking, and running computers. Many schools have adult education courses for people who are working but want to take courses in the evening.

For further information on:

Educators, *see* BETHUNE, MARY MC LEOD; MANN, HORACE; WASHINGTON, BOOKER T.

Learning, *see* PROGRAMMED LEARNING, PSYCHOLOGY, REASONING, TEACHING.

Schools, *see* COLLEGES AND UNIVERSITIES, SCHOOL.

Types of Education, *see* APPRENTICESHIP, INDUSTRIAL ARTS, PHYSICAL EDUCATION, SPECIAL EDUCATION.

▲A science student at work in school in Kenya, Africa. All over the world people are improving their lives through education.

EDWARD, KINGS OF ENGLAND Three Edwards had ruled as kings of England before the Normans of France took over the country—Edward the Elder, who ruled from 901 to 924; Edward the Martyr, who ruled from 975 to 978; and Edward the Confessor, who ruled from 1042 to 1066. Eight other Edwards have also been English kings.

Edward I (1239–1307) was one of England's greatest kings. He strengthened his government by establishing Parliament, and gave Parliament the right to pass some important laws and vote on taxes. He conquered Wales and made it part of England. He also won some battles against Scotland, but he never succeeded in conquering the Scots.

Edward II (1284–1327) was tall and handsome like his father, Edward I, but he was not a strong king. He was beaten by the Scottish leader, Robert Bruce, at the Battle of Bannockburn in 1314. He was thrown into prison by his enemies, who included his wife. His son was made king. Eight months later Edward II was murdered.

Edward III (1312–1377) became king at about age 15, when his father, Edward II, was put in prison. Edward III was a great warrior but not a great ruler. He fought the Scots, and started the Hundred Years' War with France. A plague, called the Black Death, killed thousands during his reign.

Edward IV (1442–1483) became king during the Wars of the Roses, which were between the York and Lancaster families. Edward was a York and was crowned after he defeated the Lancastrians in the Battle of Mortimer's Cross in 1461. England and France fought a war in 1475 which ended that same year when Edward made a treaty with King Louis XI of France. Louis agreed to pay a yearly tribute to England in return for peace.

Edward V (1470–1483) became king at age 12 on the death of his father, Edward IV. But he was never crowned, and he never ruled. He and his brother, Richard, were kidnapped and put in the Tower of London, where they were murdered. Some historians believe that the boys were imprisoned and murdered by their uncle, Richard, Duke of Gloucester, who then became King Richard III. But this has never been proved.

Edward VI (1537–1553) was the son of Henry VIII and Jane Seymour. He became king when he was ten. He was sickly and died at age 16. His half-sister, Mary, then became queen. His other half-sister, Elizabeth, followed Mary to the throne.

Edward VII (1841–1910) was Queen Victoria's oldest son. He was 60 when his mother died and he became king. He was a popular king who enjoyed sports, especially yachting and horse racing. Edward traveled and tried to keep peace in Europe. He was called "Edward the Peace Maker."

Edward VIII (1894–1972) reigned only 325 days and was never crowned. He gave up, or abdicated, his right to the throne to marry a divorced American woman, Mrs. Wallis Simpson. He was given the title Duke of Windsor. He served as governor of the Bahamas from 1940 to 1945.

ALSO READ: EDWARD THE CONFESSOR; ELIZABETH I; ENGLISH HISTORY; MARY, QUEENS OF ENGLAND; RICHARD, KINGS OF ENGLAND.

▲*Lady Elizabeth Grey pleads with English king Edward IV to return her land.*

▲*Edward VII, English king. He gave his name to the Edwardian Age in the early years of this century.*

▼*Edward VIII, English king who gave up the throne. He was made the Duke of Windsor.*

▲*Edward the Confessor, English king.*

EDWARD THE CONFESSOR (about 1002-1066) Edward the Confessor was born in England. But he lived in Normandy, a part of France, until he became king of England in 1042, after his half-brother, Hardecanute, died.

Edward was a weak king. He allowed his father-in-law, Godwin, Earl of the West Saxons, to make most of his decisions for him. Edward also put several of his Norman friends in important government and church positions. But the people liked Edward, and England had several years of peace during his reign. Some people believed Edward was so good that the sick could be cured by touching him.

Edward was a religious man. He founded England's famous church, Westminster Abbey. He was given the title of "Confessor" nearly 100 years after his death, when Pope Alexander III named him a saint.

Edward had no children. At first he promised to leave his throne to William, Duke of Normandy. But Harold, the son of Earl Godwin, later said that Edward, as he lay dying, had promised him the throne. William and Harold went to war to decide who would be king. Harold was killed in the Battle of Hastings in 1066, and William, called the Conqueror, became king.

ALSO READ: ENGLISH HISTORY, SAINT, WESTMINSTER ABBEY.

The female sea turtle comes to shore and lays her eggs, usually after sunset. She deposits 150 or more eggs, covers them with sand, and then returns to the sea. The eggs hatch by themselves.

EGG Did you know that you developed from an egg? Not the kind of egg you ate for breakfast, but a human egg. All female animals except single-celled animals produce eggs from which their young grow. The eggs of mammals are developed and protected in the female's body. The young are completely formed before they are *born,* or pass out of the mother's body.

The eggs most people are familiar with are the ones that the female *lays* before the young are developed. The young animal is not inside a newly laid egg. Within the egg is a cell called a *germ cell,* and a supply of food material. If a male sex cell is united with the germ cell, the egg is *fertilized.* Now the egg must

▶*A female gull* (right) *lays from two to three eggs in a nest made of grass or seaweed. She then spreads her feathers over the eggs. An opened egg* (far right) *that has been fertilized shows the developing blood vessels. Under the right conditions the germ cell in a fertile egg will develop into a baby chicken.*

be *incubated,* or kept warm and protected. Some animals keep their eggs warm by sitting on them. Others bury them in warm places. The single fertilized germ cell now divides into millions of cells to form all the parts of the young animal. When all the parts have been formed, the animal breaks or tears the shell around it. It *hatches* from the egg.

Eggs that are incubated and develop outside of the mother's body contain everything the *embryo* (developing animal) will need to grow. Break a chicken's egg into a saucer. The large yellow body is the *yolk.* The light-colored, pinhead-sized dot on the yolk is the germ cell. The yolk is the nourishment, or food, for the embryo that will develop from the germ cell. The thick transparent liquid surrounding the yolk is the egg white, or *albumen.* The albumen provides water and a soft cushion for the developing embryo.

Millions of different kinds of animals produce eggs, including fish, birds, amphibians, reptiles, and insects. The size, shape, and development of eggs vary according to the kind of animal that produces them and the conditions under which they develop. The eggshells of some animals are quite thin and fragile, while those of other animals are leathery and thick. The number of eggs an animal produces at one time varies with the eggs' chances for survival. For example, since fish eggs are often eaten by other animals, many fish lay millions of eggs at one time. Below are the number of eggs that certain kinds of female animals produce at one time. There are some variations because the number of eggs laid depends on the species of animal.

ALSO READ: BIRD, INCUBATOR, POULTRY, REPRODUCTION.

▲*Fish that do not look after their young may lay thousands and even millions of eggs all at one time. Many of the eggs are not fertilized. Fish that take care of their young produce fewer eggs.*

ANIMAL	NUMBER OF EGGS
CALIFORNIA CONDOR	1 (EVERY TWO YEARS)
PIGEON	2 (TWICE A YEAR)
HEN	210 (EVERY YEAR)
HOUSEFLY	600–1,000 (WITHIN ITS 12-DAY LIFE SPAN)
SPIDER	10–2000
SNAKE	100
TURTLE	1–200 +
FROG	25,000
HUMAN	1 (EVERY MONTH)

EGYPT   Egypt lies in the northeast corner of Africa. (See the map with the article on the MIDDLE EAST.) Its official name is Arab Republic of Egypt.

Egypt's northern boundary is the Mediterranean Sea. On the east lies Israel and 1,200 miles of the Red Sea coast. Libya lies

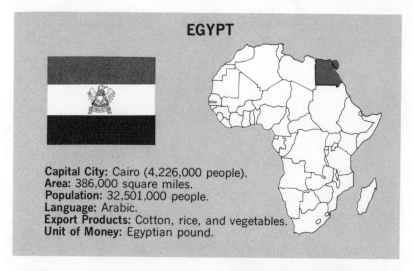

EGYPT

Capital City: Cairo (4,226,000 people).
Area: 386,000 square miles.
Population: 32,501,000 people.
Language: Arabic.
Export Products: Cotton, rice, and vegetables.
Unit of Money: Egyptian pound.

to the west and Sudan to the south. Most of Egypt is hot, dry desert, but the Nile River gives the country some fertile farm land. The billion-dollar Aswan Dam, finished in 1970, provides water for an extra one million acres of land.

Egypt is primarily an agricultural country. People raise cotton, wheat, barley, rice, citrus fruits, dates, and sugar cane. Some Egyptians are industrial workers, employed in textile and steel mills, automotive, fertilizer, and cement plants, glass factories, as well as petroleum refineries. East of the Nile River Valley lies the Suez Canal, which connects the Mediterranean and Red seas. It was a major waterway between Europe and Asia before it was closed by war in 1967.

Nobody knows where the Egyptian people came from, but written records of their history go back 6,000 years. The largest group living in Egypt today are the peasants called *fellahin,* who make up approximately three-quarters of the population. Most fellahin live in poverty. Large numbers of Arabs, Greeks, Syrians, Turks, and Armenians are part of today's population. A few are Europeans. Most Egyptians are members of the Islamic faith.

King Farouk governed Egypt between 1936 and 1952, when military officers led a bloody revolt. They took control of the government, and the king was forced to flee. Gamal Abdel Nasser was elected president in 1956. When he died in 1970, Anwar Sadat became the nation's leader.

Egypt and Israel have been enemies since 1948, when Israel was established. The Egyptians and other nations surrounding Israel feel that the land does not belong to the Israelis, who mostly come from other parts of the world. They think the Palestinians, people who have lived in present-day Israel, should have the region as their homeland. Egypt and her allies invaded the new country of Israel in 1948. They were defeated. Israeli forces took over the Sinai Peninsula in 1956, but Israel

▼ *Tomatoes grow plentifully in an area of the desert blessed by abundant ground water. Changing the desert from a barren wilderness to a fertile area is one of the major tasks of the Egyptian government.*

was forced to give up the peninsula in 1957. A full-scale war broke out in 1967, and Israel successfully defeated Egypt. An uneasy truce has existed between Egypt and Israel since then. Egypt joined with Syria and Libya in 1971 to form the Arab Republic of Egypt.

ALSO READ: AFRICA; CAIRO; EGYPT, ANCIENT; ISRAEL; MIDDLE EAST; NASSER, GAMAL ABDEL; NILE RIVER; SUEZ CANAL.

EGYPT, ANCIENT   Ancient Egypt was one of the greatest civilizations that ever existed. Its magnificent history began over 5,000 years ago and lasted almost 3,000 years. Ancient historians whose writings were preserved tell us much about ancient Egypt's civilization. What the historians say is also proved by the mighty ruins the Egyptians left behind.

People have lived in the Nile River Valley since before 5000 B.C. They settled mainly in two areas, the Nile Valley, which became Upper Egypt, and the Nile Delta (mouth of the river), or Lower Egypt. Egypt's greatness began when these two lands were joined under a single king. Scholars divide the history of Ancient Egypt into three main periods, called the Old Kingdom, the Middle Kingdom, and the New Kingdom.

▼*A wooden statue of Sesostri I, a ruler of the twelfth dynasty of the Middle Kingdom. The stiff, formal pose is typical of the Ancient Egyptian sculpture.*

The Three Kingdoms

The Old Kingdom lasted from about 3100 B.C. to about 2242 B.C. It began when, according to tradition, a king named Menes united Upper and Lower Egypt into one nation. He founded the city of Memphis as his capital. Menes started the first Egyptian *dynasty* (a line of rulers in the same family). Kings in Egypt were called *pharaoh,* which meant "great house." Egypt's greatest pyramids were built during the time of the Old Kingdom. The pyramids were immense tombs (burial places) for the kings of Egypt. They were made of huge blocks of stone built up in steps and rising to a point at the top. The Great Pyramids of Giza may still be seen today. The base of the largest pyramid covers 13 acres. The Great Sphinx, a giant stone figure with the body of a lion and the head of a man, lies near the pyramids.

The Egyptians developed a brilliant civilization during this time. They created impressive paintings and sculpture. They made studies of the stars and planets and invented a calendar with a 365-day year. The accurate measurements used for building the pyramids show that they were skilled in mathematics and engineering. The Egyptians also developed new ideas about medicine and surgery. Eight dynasties ruled during the period of the Old Kingdom. Towards the end of this period, Egypt was weakened by constant battles for power among nobles, priests, and the pharaohs.

The Middle Kingdom lasted from about 2242 B.C. to about 1567 B.C. Nine dynasties ruled during this time. A nobleman of

TABLE OF ANCIENT EGYPT'S HISTORY

Prehistory	Before 3400 B.C.
Old Kingdom (Dynasties I through VIII)	3100–2242 B.C.
Middle Kingdom (Dynasties IX through XVII)	2242–1567 B.C.
New Kingdom (Dynasties XVIII through XXX)	1567–332 B.C.
Ptolemy Period	332–30 B.C.
Roman Period	30 B.C.–395 A.D.
Byzantine Period	395–640 A.D.

The Great Pyramid of Cheops in Giza, Egypt, is composed of more than two million blocks of stone, which weigh an average of 2½ tons each. The pyramid is 446 feet high and covers about 12 acres.

the city of Thebes founded a dynasty around 2160 B.C. that brought prosperity and growth to Egypt once again. Architecture, art, and literature flourished. A canal was built between the Nile River and the Red Sea. Around 1680 B.C. barbaric invaders, called the *Hyksos,* overran Egypt. The Hyksos fought with horses, horse-drawn chariots, and bronze weapons. These fighting methods were new to the Egyptians, but they soon learned how to use the new weapons. One hundred years later the Egyptians drove out the Hyksos.

The New Kingdom lasted from about 1567 to about 332 B.C. Egypt enjoyed its last great period of splendor during these years. Thirteen dynasties ruled during this time. Thutmose III, a member of the eighteenth dynasty, made Egypt into a powerful empire. Amenhotep IV became pharaoh around 1370 B.C. His queen was the beautiful Nefertiti.

The Egyptians had always believed in many gods. Their pharaohs were thought to be gods, too, and had enormous power. Amenhotep IV ordered his subjects to worship only Ra, the sun god. He changed Ra's name to Aton, an ancient name for Ra. He also changed his own name to Ikhnaton, meaning "Aton is satisfied." But the Egyptians were unhappy without their traditional gods. After Ikhnaton's death, the pharaoh Tutankhamen allowed the people to return to their old ways of worship. Another pharaoh, Ramses II, built the colossal temple of Abu Simbel around 1250 B.C.

In the last years of the New Kingdom, Egypt was overrun by invaders. Libyans and the Assyrians ruled the country. The Persians captured Egypt in 525 B.C. Alexander the Great conquered

▶*The Egyptian mummy shown here is a body that was preserved after death and wrapped in cloth. The mummy is wearing a mask. It was buried in this painted wooden box, inside a stone tomb.*

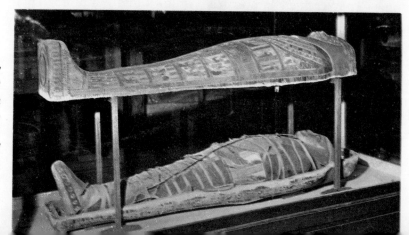

Great Architectural Achievements of the Ancient Egyptians	
The Old Kingdom	
Dynasty (B.C.)	**Achievement**
I and II 3100–2780	Memphis was built, the first capital of ancient Egypt. It stood near the site of Cairo, the capital of modern Egypt.
III 2780–2680	The first pyramid, the Step Pyramid, was designed during the reign of Zoser.
IV 2680–2560	The three Great Pyramids were built at Giza. The Sphinx was built near the second pyramid. It was probably built to protect nearby tombs from evil spirits.
The New Kingdom	
Dynasty (B.C.)	**Achievement**
XVIII 1567–1320	A splendid temple was built at Deir el-Bahri near Thebes. It honors Hatshepsut, the first great queen known to history. Tomb of Tutankhamen was an immense display of jewelry and art. It was built near Luxor, one of the first great cities of the ancient world. It was not discovered until 1922.
XIX 1320–1200	The two great temples of Abu Simbel were built during the reign of the famous ruler, Ramses II. The great temple was carved 200 feet into the side of a mountain. The splendid temple of Amon-Re was also built during his reign to honor the main god of ancient Egypt. Beautiful painted columns decorated its great hall.

Egypt in 332 B.C. and founded the city of Alexandria.

After Alexander's death in 323 B.C., Ptolemy named himself king of Egypt. Ptolemy's dynasty ended with the death of Queen Cleopatra in 30 B.C. In the same year, the Romans captured Egypt and added it to their empire. When the Roman Empire split in two in 395 A.D., the Byzantine emperors controlled Egypt. Christianity became widespread in Egypt between 300 and 500 A.D. but did not last. In the 640s, an Arab general conquered Egypt, and it became a Muslim country.

The Egyptians and Their Accomplishments

Most of the people in ancient Egypt lived near the Nile River. Its yearly flooding deposited rich, black soil which was excellent

▲ *An example of hiero-*
glyphics on papyrus, a type
of paper. It is from the
Book of the Dead, written to
aid the soul on its journey
into the afterlife.

for farming. Egyptian traders traveled by sea and caravan all over the parts of the world known then. The Egyptians developed a system of picture-writing called *hieroglyphics.* They also made writing paper from the *papyrus* reed. Scholars have been able to read hieroglyphics ever since the famous *Rosetta Stone* was discovered and interpreted in the early 1800s.

The Egyptians believed in a life after death. They placed many objects, such as food, clothing, and doll-like figures of servants, in their tombs. This was to make the afterlife more pleasant. They wrapped their dead in layers of cloth and preserved them as mummies, many of which can be seen in museums today. One of the Egyptians' most powerful gods was Osiris, god of the dead. They also worshiped many animal gods, including bulls, crocodiles, and cats. The Egyptians built mighty temples and statues of stone to honor their god-pharaohs. Long after the Egyptian civilization had disappeared, people looked back and marveled at the achievements of that ancient world—the Land of the Pharaohs.

Many ancient Egyptians were farmers. Originally they owned their own land. As time passed, the farms became the property of nobles and pharaohs. The farmers raised crops of wheat, barley, flax, and grapes on irrigated land. They also raised cattle. Other Egyptians were craftsmen, working with clay, stone, and different metals to make jars, bowls, jewelry, and tools. Some wove linen and other materials. Other Egyptians were soldiers. Most Egyptians lived in clay huts with flat roofs made from reeds or palm branches. They were sparsely furnished with wooden stools and reed mats on the floors. Egyptians ate bread (made from wheat or barley), fish, and vegetables. Their favorite beverage was a drink made from grain that was very much like beer.

ALSO READ: ABU SIMBEL, ANCIENT CIVILIZATIONS, BYZANTINE EMPIRE, CALENDAR, CLEOPATRA, DOLL, EGYPT, PYRAMID, ROSETTA STONE, SPHINX.

EINSTEIN, ALBERT (1879–1955) Albert Einstein, one of the most brilliant scientists of all time, was born in Ulm, Germany. As a boy, Einstein was a poor student, but he was destined to change man's concept of nature and the universe.

Einstein was a founder of a new branch of physics, called *relativity.* In the 1600s, Sir Isaac Newton set forth what have become known as the laws of motion. These rules describe how objects move and explain the forces that cause motion. In his "Special Theory of Relativity," published in 1905, Einstein predicted that objects moving at nearly the speed of light (about 186,000 miles a second) do not obey Newton's laws. In the years since Einstein announced his ideas, many physicists have developed machines for studying the tiny bits of matter that make up atoms. All these particles—which move at terrific speeds—have shown that Einstein's theory is correct. This theory showed that matter and energy are really two different forms of the same thing. A small piece of matter can be changed into a huge amount of energy. The truth of this bold new idea blazed into reality with the creation and explosion of the first atomic bomb in 1945. Einstein was very sad when he learned that atomic bombs had been dropped on Japan. He was a peaceful man who hated war. Einstein spent the last years of his life urging mankind to use atomic energy for peaceful purposes.

Einstein published his "General Theory of Relativity" in 1915. This theory tries to explain gravitation. Scientists are still testing the theory. It is one of the greatest triumphs of the human mind. In 1921, Einstein was awarded the Nobel Prize in physics. He left Germany when Adolf Hitler began restricting the activities of Jews. In the 1930s, Einstein became a citizen of the United States. He became director of mathematics at the Institute for Advanced Studies in Princeton, New Jersey. He worked there for the rest of his life. All of his research was aimed at developing a theory that would explain the effects of both electromagnetism and gravitation.

ALSO READ: ATOM; GRAVITY AND GRAVITATION; LIGHT; NEWTON, SIR ISAAC; NUCLEAR ENERGY; RELATIVITY; SCIENCE.

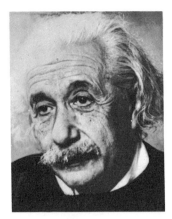

▲ *Albert Einstein.*

EISENHOWER, DWIGHT DAVID (1890–1969) The thirty-fourth President of the United States, Dwight Eisenhower, was one of the most popular American leaders of modern times. He was a cheerful, smiling man. His nickname was "Ike." Many of his friends and admirers wore buttons that said, "I like Ike."

Dwight Eisenhower was born in Denison, Texas, and grew up in Abilene, Kansas. His parents named him David Dwight, but he always called himself Dwight. After he graduated from high school, he went to the United States Military Academy at West Point, New York, where he studied to be an army officer. He graduated in 1915 and became a second lieutenant in the army.

Eisenhower worked hard during the years that followed. He served as a member of General Douglas McArthur's staff in the Philippines. He was promoted many times. Eisenhower planned the Louisiana Maneuvers—special training operations held just before the U.S. entered World War II. The maneuvers went so well that high-ranking army officers noticed him. He was a brigadier general in 1941 when the United States entered the war.

The United States and its allies had to invade Europe to win the war. Everyone knew this would be very difficult because the German army was very strong. President Franklin Roosevelt and General George Marshall searched for the right man to command the invasion. Eisenhower got the job. He became

▼ *While Eisenhower was President, the United States began to explore space. The first U.S. satellite, Explorer I, was placed in orbit on January 31, 1958. A model of it is shown here.*

THIRTY-FOURTH PRESIDENT   JANUARY 21, 1953—JANUARY 20, 1961

Born: October 14, 1890, Denison, Texas
Parents: David Jacob and Ida Elizabeth Stoever (or Stover) Eisenhower
Education: United States Military Academy, West Point, New York
Religion: Presbyterian
Occupation: Army officer
Political Party: Republican
Married: 1916 to Mamie Geneva Doud Eisenhower (born 1896)
Children: 2 sons (one died as a child)
Died: March 28, 1969, Washington, D.C.
Buried: Eisenhower Center Chapel, Abilene, Kansas

DWIGHT DAVID EISENHOWER

commander of all the Allied troops in Europe in 1942. Eisenhower worked with military leaders from many countries to plan the invasion. The invasion was successful. But months of hard fighting followed before Nazi Germany surrendered in May, 1945.

Eisenhower was promoted to five-star general in 1944. After the war he served as president of Columbia University from 1948 to 1950. He became commander of the North Atlantic Treaty Organization (NATO) forces in 1950.

Many people wanted Eisenhower to be President of the United States. The Republican Party nominated him in 1952. He won the election and was re-elected in 1956. President Eisenhower worked hard to bring about world peace. He visited many foreign countries to bring about better understanding among the peoples of the world.

ALSO READ: WORLD WAR II.

EL DORADO   When the Spaniards first came to South America, they heard the legend of El Dorado, which means "the gilded man" in Spanish. The legend probably described the Chibcha Indians of Colombia. It was said that once a year their chief would cover his body with sacred oil and gold dust. Then he would dive into a special lake to wash off the gold. His people would toss gold and emeralds into the lake. The chief became known as El Dorado, and later his village and country acquired the name. Many explorers went to hunt for the fabled golden city, which was sometimes called Monoa. Francisco de Orellana led an expedition in search of El Dorado in 1541. Sir Walter Raleigh set out to look for it in 1595. No one ever found the golden city. Today the name is used to describe any place of legendary riches and wealth.

ALSO READ: CONQUISTADOR; EXPLORATION; RALEIGH, SIR WALTER.

ELEANOR OF AQUITAINE (about 1122-1204) Eleanor of Aquitaine was a beautiful French princess who married two kings and was the mother of two more kings. She was born in the province of Aquitaine in southwestern France.

Eleanor was first married at 15 to a prince who, a month later, became King Louis VII of France. They had two daughters. Eleanor and Louis were later divorced. Then, in 1152, Eleanor married Henry Plantagenet. He became Henry II of England two years later. Henry and Eleanor had three daughters and five sons.

Eleanor and her sons tried to seize the throne from Henry in 1173. But Henry put down their revolt and forced Eleanor to live in a convent until he released her in 1185. Eleanor made certain that Richard, who was her favorite son, would become the next king. When Henry died in 1189, Richard did become king. He was called Richard the Lion-Hearted because he was a great warrior. During his reign, he went on a crusade to the Holy Land for several years. His mother ruled in his place until he returned. She also kept her son John from seizing the throne.

Eleanor lived a long life—long enough to see Richard die and John become king. She acted as John's adviser until her death at age 82.

ALSO READ: CRUSADES; ENGLISH HISTORY; HENRY, KINGS OF ENGLAND; JOHN, KING OF ENGLAND; LOUIS, KINGS OF FRANCE; RICHARD, KINGS OF ENGLAND.

ELECTION Every year the members of Mrs. Brown's class choose a new president. The president conducts class meetings. This year both John and Anne want to be president. Some of the class members want Anne for president. Others want John. To decide who will be president, the class holds an *election*.

In the election, everyone who is a member of the class has one *vote* (he can make only one selection for the office of president). Each member writes the name of the person he or she wants to be president on a slip of paper. The slip of paper is called a *ballot*. No one is supposed to see the name someone writes on the ballot, because the vote is secret. Each class member puts a ballot in a special box called the *ballot box*. After everyone has voted, the ballots are counted. Anne has the most votes and she wins the election. She becomes president of the class.

Thousands and thousands of elections are held in the United States each year. Clubs, societies, labor unions, and companies all hold elections. In these elections, members decide who will be in charge of those groups. The people who own stock in companies elect directors to run the companies.

Most officials who run our country are elected. In most cities or towns any adult living there may vote for the mayor, council-

▼*An election official empties out the ballot box to count the votes in a British election.*

men, aldermen, or selectmen and for other officials who will govern the community. Citizens of your state vote for the governor, members of the state legislature, and the other officials who will run the state. A citizen also votes for the President of the United States and for the representatives and senators who will represent your state in the United States Congress.

In order to vote in a city election, a person must live in the city. A person voting in a state election must live in the state. He must be an American citizen and be able to read and write. The 26th Amendment to the Constitution, ratified on June 30, 1971, lowered the voting age from 21 to 18 years.

Before someone can actually vote, he must *register* to vote. He goes to a special office for voter registration and proves to the people there that he meets the qualifications. He also tells the people in this office where he lives and how long he has lived there. Sometimes, they may have the person take a reading test to make sure he will be able to read the ballot. They then put the new voter's name in a large book called an *election register*. A voter can register as a member of the Democratic or Republican party. If he prefers, he can register as an independent voter. If he registers as a party member, he can vote in that party's *primary* election. In a primary election, the members of a political party vote to choose the party's candidates for the general election. Such an election is held before the regular election. Election Day for the office of President and Vice President of the United States is held on the first Tuesday after the first Monday in November, once every four years. States and communities hold elections every two years or every year. The dates of these elections are stated in special laws.

When election day comes, a person goes to the polling place in his neighborhood. The polling place may be a room in a school, a police station, or even in someone's home. Small booths with curtains in front of them are put up to make sure each voter makes his choices in secret. The polling place is run by special election officials. The voter signs the register to prove he came to the polling place to vote. The election official gives the voter a ballot, and he takes it into the booth. The person closes the curtain of the booth behind him, and votes for whomever he wants. When he comes out of the booth, he puts the ballot into a special ballot box. Some communities use voting machines instead of ballots. The voter presses levers on the voting machine to signal his choices.

While each person is voting, election officials perform other duties. They make sure each voter does not take too much time in the booth. They do not allow people to tell voters how to mark their ballots.

After the polling places close, all the votes are counted in a central place. As various election results are known, they are

A ballot printed on one kind of paper listing all candidates in an election was first used in Australia in 1856. Before that, each candidate furnished his own style of ballot. Voters could not keep their choice secret. This uniform ballot is still called the *Australian ballot*.

announced on radio and television. More up-to-date results appear in the newspapers the next day. The candidates who have won the largest number of votes are elected.

Elections in other countries differ from those held in the United States. Each government decides what the qualifications are to become a voter. In some countries, such as Liechtenstein, only men can vote. In other countries, a dictator and his political party are in charge. They choose the candidates they want to run for office. No other candidates' names appear on the ballot.

ALSO READ: GOVERNMENT, POLITICAL PARTY.

ELECTRIC APPLIANCE Look around your home and count the number of appliances that depend upon electricity. Electric appliances provide light, heat, and refrigeration. They do work for us. Power saws, drills, and other electric tools help us do chores quickly and better. Electricity improves our lives in so many ways that it would probably take a whole book just to list them. We enjoy good health, talk to friends around the world, and avoid many kinds of difficult work, all because of machines that run on electricity.

Electric appliances can be divided into two different types that depend on two different characteristics of electricity. (1) Electricity produces heat or heat and light when it flows through certain wires called resistance wires. (2) Flowing electricity has a magnetic field around it, which makes possible electric motors.

When electricity flows through resistance wires, heat or heat and light are produced. *Resistance wires* "resist" or oppose the flow of electricity, and they get hot when electricity passes through them. Some resistance wires resist electricity so strongly that they become white hot. These wires are used for making light bulbs. Appliances which use electricity to make heat or light include toasters, electric stoves, heaters, electric blankets, irons, hotplates, electric frying pans, fluorescent lights, and ordinary lights. The flat wires along the sides of a toaster are resistance wires. You can see them glow red and you can feel their heat when the toaster is operating. Never touch these wires with your fingers or any piece of metal, such as a knife, or you will receive a bad shock.

Many people believe that the invention of the electric light is one of man's greatest achievements. Thomas Alva Edison succeeded in making the first commercial electric light in 1879. He worked for over a year trying different materials to use as a filament. The *filament* is the thread-like wire in an electric bulb. When electric current passes through a filament, so much heat is produced that the filament gets white hot and glows with a brilliant light. Metal filaments will burn in air, so an inert gas

▲*An electric toothbrush is a useful appliance for massaging the gums and brushing the teeth effectively. This one runs on batteries.*

▼*A modern light bulb showing the tungsten filament.*

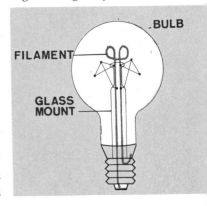

(one which does not react easily) must be put into the bulb. Most light bulbs today have tungsten filaments in a bulb containing an inert mixture of argon and nitrogen gases. A tungsten light bulb is a simple device. A glass bulb, a filament, and a screw-in base are the main parts. You can see in the drawing how such a light bulb is made.

Electric Motors

The opposite of resistance wires are *conduction wires,* which conduct (carry) electricity very easily and produce very little heat. Conduction wires are essential in all appliances that have electric motors, such as vacuum cleaners, washing machines, air conditioners, fans, sewing machines, mixers, power tools, and many others.

An electric motor contains two electromagnets. One electromagnet is wrapped around a shaft (axle) that can turn. The other electromagnet is held in place. When the motor is on—when electric current enters the motor—the electromagnet on the shaft is pulled around and around by the fixed electromagnet. The shaft must turn as the electromagnet does, and the shaft is connected to the moving parts of the appliance. You can see how the shaft of a fan is connected to the blades.

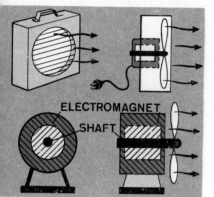

▲*Structure of the motor-controlled shaft of an electric fan.*

You can do a simple experiment that shows how the magnetism of an electric motor works. This experiment was first done by Hans Oersted, a Danish scientist, 150 years ago. Oersted proved that an electrical current moving through a wire produces magnetism.

To do Oersted's experiment, you will need a piece of insulated copper wire, a dry cell, and a pocket compass. Connect one end of the wire to one of the battery terminals. Lay the wire across the top of the compass, and touch the other end of the wire to the other battery terminal. (Do NOT use uninsulated wire.) What happens to the compass needle? It moves because it is a magnet brought near another magnet—the wire carrying electricity. An electric motor operates in the same way.

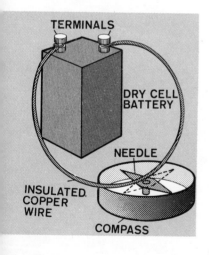

Electrical appliances are often said to be labor-saving devices. You can see the reason for this if you think about doing the laundry. For thousands of years, this meant hard work. A fire had to be built. Water had to be carried from the well and heated over the fire. Each piece of laundry had to be washed by hand, rinsed by hand, squeezed, and hung up to dry. The laundry for a family took hours to do. Today, you can put all your laundry into a washer-dryer, add soap, and turn on the switch. In an hour or less, the whole family's laundry is clean, dry, and ready to wear.

When a lot of current is being used to operate many appliances, the wires that carry electricity to all the rooms of a house can get so hot that they cause a fire. This is prevented by one of two special devices, a fuse or a circuit breaker. A *fuse* is a thin strip of metal that is placed in the path of the electric current. When the electric wires become hot or "overloaded," the fuse melts and stops the flow of electricity. Without a fuse, electrical appliances can cause fires. With a fuse, these devices are not dangerous. Look closely at a fuse and you can see the strip of metal that melts to prevent the electric wires from getting too hot.

A *circuit breaker* is a special kind of switch. When it is "on," current flows through it. But attached to the switch is a device that measures the current. If the current gets too strong, the device throws the switch and stops the current. Many modern buildings use circuit breakers instead of fuses.

Appliances in Our World

Many appliances start out as luxuries, but people soon think they are necessary. Refrigerators, for example, were considered a luxury when they first came into use. Do you think you could get along well without a refrigerator? Where would you get a cold drink on a hot day? Where would you keep ice cream? When our lights go out in a thunderstorm, we scurry around looking for candles and flashlights until the electricity comes on again. Electric lights, along with many other appliances, have become necessary in modern industrial countries. Scientists and engineers work constantly to improve appliances. New designs are tested, and improvements are made on existing designs. Appliances that people need and want are manufactured in great numbers.

Appliances usually come with a set of instructions. These instructions should always be saved because they tell how the appliance should be operated and cared for. With proper care, most appliances last for years.

ALSO READ: ELECTRICITY, ELECTRIC POWER, ELECTRONICS, LIGHTING, MAGNET, MOTOR.

▲*Switching devices such as these regulate the flow of electricity. For example, if people are using too much electricity, the supply can be automatically reduced through these devices.*

ELECTRICITY Men have known about the form of energy called electricity for a very long time. The ancient Greeks knew that if they rubbed the material called amber with fur, the amber would attract bits of dust and straw. The Greek word for "amber" was *elektron,* from which the word "electricity" comes.

You know that electricity lights your house. It may also heat—and cool—your house, and refrigerate—and cook—your food. Electricity carries your friend's voice to you on the telephone, brings your favorite TV show to you, and operates your phonograph.

What is electricity? No one knows. "Electricity" is what we call something that no man has ever seen—"electricity" is a mystery. Don't we feel electricity when we get a shock? Don't we sometimes see it flash? The answer to both of these questions is, "No." We can only see, feel, and hear the things that electricity does. When an electric spark crackles, you are seeing a flash and hearing a sound made by electricity. *No man has ever seen, felt, or heard electricity itself.*

Electricity does not happen just for man to use, however. Electricity is constantly produced in the stars, in space, and in Earth's atmosphere. Electric signals jump from nerve cell to nerve cell in the bodies of animals. A few animals stun their prey with strong electric currents. Everything in the universe depends on electricity. All matter is built of atoms, and electricity holds the parts of every atom together.

Electrical energy is carried by electrons, the tiny particles that combine with neutrons and protons to form atoms. An electron is a *very* tiny particle. If you could collect electrons, you would have to collect 2,550,800,000,000,000,000,000,000,000,000 of them to have enough to weigh one ounce! Electrons may have either a positive or a negative electrical charge. The electrons that orbit the nucleus of an atom have negative charges, and these are the electrons that we usually deal with. A *positron* is a particle that weighs exactly as much as an electron, but has a positive electrical charge. The positron—"positive electron"—is produced under special circumstances, such as when X-rays crash into atoms.

Two Kinds of Electricity

People sometimes talk about static electricity and current electricity. These are really two forms of the same thing—electrons —but it is sometimes convenient to talk about them separately. *Static electricity* consists of electrons that are not moving. *Current electricity* consists of electrons in motion.

STATIC ELECTRICITY. Rub a balloon several times against your hair or against a wool sweater. The balloon picks up electrons from your hair—becomes negatively charged—and will stick against a wall, which is not charged. Static electricity may give you a shock when you walk across a carpet and then touch another person or a metal door or radiator.

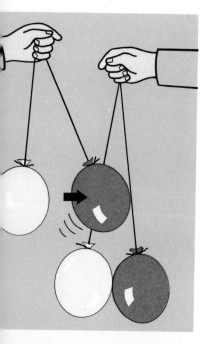

You can use static electricity to see one of the basic characteristics of electricity. You will need two small inflated balloons tied to long pieces of string and a small piece of wool. First rub one of the balloons with the wool. Then hold the ends of both pieces of string in your hand and let the balloons dangle. What happens? Now rub the other balloon with wool, too, and let the balloons dangle again. What happens this time? The balloons push apart because both balloons are negatively charged and similar charges repel each other. What happens if you rub one balloon with wool and the other with silk or nylon? Does this make any difference?

CURRENT ELECTRICITY. Current electricity can also make objects stick together or give you a shock. But current electricity has uses that have made enormous changes in people's lives.

Current electricity moves through certain substances called *conductors*. Conductors conduct electricity because they contain free electrons that can move from atom to atom. Most metals contain many free electrons and make good conductors. Silver is the best conductor in most cases. But silver is so expensive that the second-best conductor—copper—is usually used instead. Some substances have almost no free electrons. Almost all the electrons are held very tightly in their orbits. These substances, such as air, glass, and rubber, are called *insulators* or *nonconductors*. The cords that carry electric current from the wall plugs to the appliances in your home consist of copper (or aluminum) wires to conduct the current and a rubber "envelope" to protect you from shock. Current electricity can be produced with a machine called a *generator*.

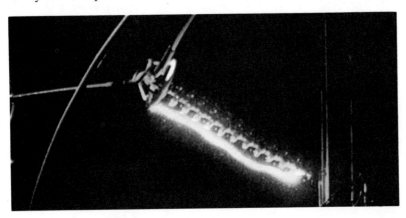

◄*Electricity can be transmitted through high power lines. Here, a flash of electricity occurs over an insulation device.*

How Electricity Moves

It does not take long for a light bulb to glow when you turn it on. It does not take long for you to feel the shock if you accidentally touch a wire that is carrying current. How fast is electricity? This question has more than one answer. When electricity flows through a wire, the electrons move from atom to atom at a speed of a few feet a second. But the electric *signal* moves almost at the speed of light—186,000 miles a second.

You can get an idea of how this signal travels through a wire. Make a straight line of five or six checkers or coins, so that each piece touches the next in the line. Put one finger on top of the second checker. Then, with your other hand, slide the first checker back a few inches and bang it straight into the checker you are holding in place. The checkers in the line do not move very much, but the last one shoots ahead. Electrons in a conductor act something like this line of checkers. The electrons do not move very quickly, but when one end of the "line" of electrons is pushed, they send a very rapid signal down the line to

▶*Try to imagine the millions of atoms that make up a conducting wire. Loosely held electrons* (shown in red) *move from one atom to the next, where they push other electrons on to the next atom. They are attracted by the positive charges* (shown in blue) *at the end of the circuit. Along the way, the current of negative charges lights the light bulb.*

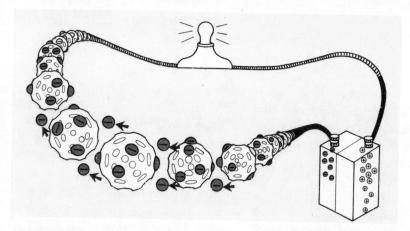

the other end. For this reason, you see (and feel) the effects of electricity at once.

Current electricity is related to magnetism. Watch a compass needle during a thunderstorm. Each time lightning flashes nearby, the compass needle will vibrate rapidly or swing around to point in the wrong direction for a moment or two. When current flows through a wire, a magnetic field develops around the wire. A current moving through a wire coil produces a magnetic field like that of a bar magnet. This electromagnetism is the basis of the electric motor, which uses the force of two electromagnets to produce work.

Measuring Electricity

Electricity can be measured in many ways. One machine for measuring small electric current is called a *galvanometer.* The four most common measuring units are volts, amperes, ohms, and watts.

VOLTS. Volts are units of force. Voltage is the force that causes electricity to flow. You can "see" how voltage works if you think of water in a pipe. To make the water move, a pump must work. Take away the pump, and the flow of water stops. It takes work to push electrons through a wire "pipe," too. Take away the battery or other power source, and the electron flow stops. Electrons move through a wire only if there is a difference in voltage, or *potential,* between one end of the wire and the other end. This difference is measured in units called volts. The current that operates appliances in your house is 110-volt current. A flashlight battery produces 1½-volt current. Most automobile batteries produce 12-volt current.

AMPERES. It is often useful to measure the "size" of the current. Current is measured in units called amperes, or amps. A wire is carrying a 1-amp current if 6,240,000,000,000,000,000 electrons pass any point in the wire in 1 second. In the same piece of wire, doubling the voltage—using a 3-volt battery instead of a 1½-volt battery, for example—doubles the current.

OHMS. Electric motors get hot. If a lamp is left on for a long time, you can feel the heat of the copper wires that carry current to it, even through the rubber covering. These things happen because electrons crash into atoms of the conductor. The better the conductor, the less often collisions happen. But no conductor is perfect. This is called *resistance* and is measured in ohms. Other things affect resistance, including the temperature of the conductor, its thickness, and its length.

WATTS. Watts measure power, or how quickly electricity is generated or used. If you know the voltage and current of an electric circuit, you can find the wattage by multiplying these two figures together. For example, a light bulb of about .909 amps connected to a 110-volt current uses .909 $\times$ 110 = 100 watts.

For further information on:

Basic Principles of Electricity, *see* ATOM, BATTERY, ELECTRIC POWER, ELECTRONICS, ENERGY, LIGHTNING AND THUNDER, MAGNET.

History of Electricity, *see* AMBER; AMPERE, ANDRE MARIE; EDISON, THOMAS ALVA; FARADAY, MICHAEL; GALVANI, LUIGI; WATT, JAMES.

Some Uses of Electricity, *see* ELECTRIC APPLIANCE, MOTOR, RADIO, TAPE RECORDER, TELEVISION, X-RAY.

ELECTRIC POWER Human physical strength was the first form of power known to man. With his own physical strength, man has accomplished many great deeds. But human strength was not enough to do all the things men wanted to do. It was not fast enough or strong enough. So man had to find other forms of power. Man has made use of animals, simple tools, water, and many other things to do his work for him. One of the greatest aids to man has been electricity. An electric power plant is a sort of factory because it produces a product, electricity, from some other material, such as running water. Electric power plants use generators to produce electricity. A *generator* is a device that turns mechanical energy into electrical energy. A generator may be only large enough to supply power to one house, or it may provide electricity for thousands of buildings.

The first power generators produced *direct current* (DC), a steady flow of electrons in just one direction. Flashlight batteries produce DC. Direct current is used in metal plating, in *electrolysis*—breaking down compounds into elements—and in many metal-making processes.

Alternating current (AC) flows rapidly back and forth. The current supplied to most houses is called "60-cycle AC," which means that it is alternating current that flows back and forth 60 times a second. The main reason that AC is used so widely is that losses of electrical energy over long distance transmission lines are much lower than with DC. It is also easier to change the voltage of AC. Voltage is the force that pushes electricity along. Alternating current can be "piped" hundreds of miles at a very high voltage so that little power is lost. Then the voltage can be lowered so that electric appliances will work properly.

"Making" Electricity

The simplest kind of generator is a loop of wire that can be turned. The loop is placed between the poles of a magnet, as you can see in the diagram. Whenever magnetic lines of force are cut by a wire, electric current is produced in the wire. This is the principle of the electric power generator. A generator with one loop of wire would not produce very much electricity. The generators in a power plant have a coil containing thousands of loops of wire in place of a single loop, and magnets of great strength are used to increase the power output.

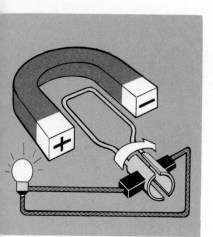

Several types of energy are used to turn the coils of wire in a generator. Many power plants produce electricity from running water. Such plants, called *hydroelectric* plants, generate nearly one-third of the world's electric power. Heat may be used where there is no falling water. Coal, gas, or wood may be burned to heat water to produce steam, which turns the generator. Nuclear reactors may also be used to produce such heat. About 100 such power plants are in operation or are under construction. Devices to produce electricity directly from the heat of nuclear reaction are now in the experimental stage.

Other devices used to turn small generators include horses, windmills, and water wheels. Solar batteries are also used. They can use sunlight to make electric power for orbiting satellites.

Electricity produced in a power plant goes from the generator through a device called a *step-up transformer*. The transformer increases the voltage from 15,000 or 20,000 volts to 220,000 volts or more. Then the electricity is pushed along wires stretched between tall towers. You have probably seen such power lines. At each tower is a sign that says DANGER! HIGH VOLTAGE. Power lines may cross hundreds of miles of open country to reach a city. At the city, the electricity goes to sub-stations, places where *step-down transformers* lower the voltage to about 15,000 volts. Other power lines then carry the electricity throughout the city, to buildings, streetlights, and wherever else electric power is needed. Near each power user is another step-down transformer, which lowers the voltage again to 110 volts (220 volts in many countries). In the drawing, you can see the path that electricity follows every day to reach your home.

ALSO READ: BATTERY, ELECTRIC APPLIANCE, ELECTRICITY, ENERGY, NUCLEAR ENERGY.

electric
power

Electricity may be produced by a hydroelectric plant (*right*). The water stored behind a dam (1) falls at great pressure (2). It spins turbines (3), which are connected by shafts (4) to generators (5). Voltage is increased for transmission, then decreased for use.

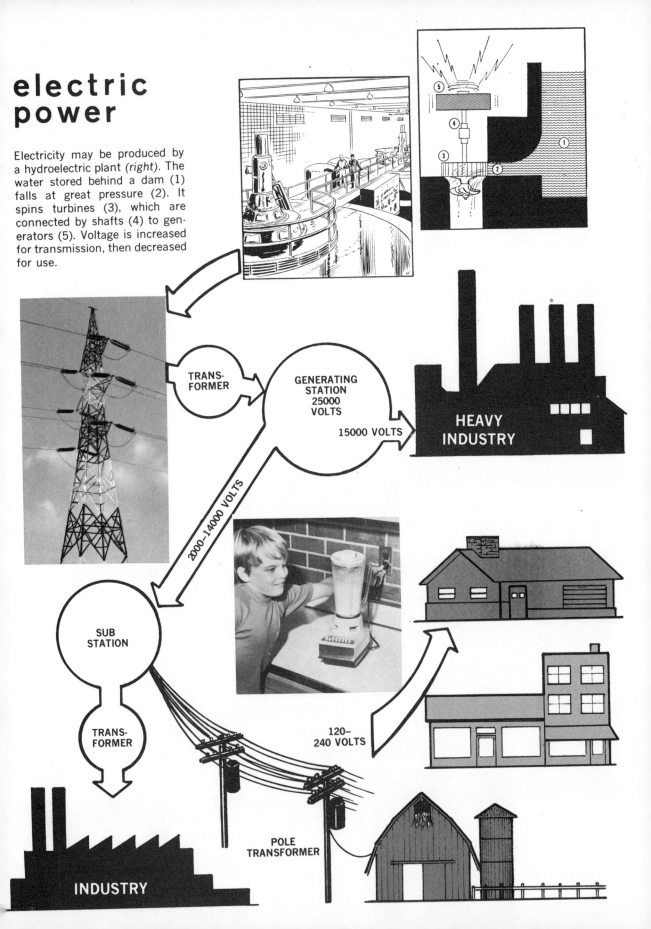

TRANS-FORMER

GENERATING STATION 25000 VOLTS

15000 VOLTS

HEAVY INDUSTRY

2000–14000 VOLTS

SUB STATION

TRANS-FORMER

120–240 VOLTS

POLE TRANSFORMER

INDUSTRY

▲*An electronic music synthesizer can make very unusual sounds as well as imitate the sounds of any musical instrument. The musician connects wires from the keys on the keyboard to the large boxes. Connecting the wires one way may make sounds like a trumpet. Connecting them another way may make the sounds of a windstorm.*

ELECTRONIC MUSIC If you have ever gone to a concert, you know that every musician must play his instrument at exactly the right moment. You also know that a trumpet always sounds like a trumpet, and never like a violin. A snare drum does not sound like a piccolo.

But there is an electronic instrument, the *synthesizer,* that differs in two ways from more familiar instruments. First, the synthesizer can imitate the sound of any other musical instrument—a guitar, a harmonica, a clarinet, a bell, or any other. The synthesizer can also make sounds no other musical instrument has ever made, such as wailing, scratching, whistling, and ticking sounds, plus sounds that cannot even be described with familiar words.

Second, a synthesizer can be connected to a computer. This means that the musician can play his instrument long before a concert, because the computer can play the instrument again at the right time.

The musician can sit in the audience and listen to the concert. He can even be hundreds of miles away, eating dinner or taking a nap. But the synthesizer is a difficult instrument. It must be played, like any other instrument, by someone who knows music and has the skill to play his instrument properly.

Composers sometimes write music for synthesizers, instead of for the older instruments. To do this, a composer decides what sounds he wants in his music. Then he figures out how to make the synthesizer play the sounds.

Composers can also write music for synthesizers plus other instruments. And many familiar instruments have been built with electronic parts. You know how different the electronic organ of a rock band sounds from the older pipe organ, such as the one religious music is often played on. Electronics has created many such new sounds from old instruments. Some composers, such as John Cage, combine these new sounds with tape-recorded sounds and voices.

ALSO READ: COMPUTER, ELECTRONICS, MODERN MUSIC, MUSIC, MUSICAL INSTRUMENTS.

ELECTRONICS   You can listen to a little radio at the beach. On television, you can see and hear about the wonderful travels of the astronauts. But do you know what science has produced the discoveries and inventions that make these amazing things possible? The science is *electronics,* the science concerned with the flow and control of electrons in vacuum tubes, transistors, and other special devices. Electrical appliances such as toasters, vacuum tubes, transistors, and light bulbs are *not* electronic devices, because in such devices the electrons are carried through wires. Some familiar devices that depend on electronics are radio, television, tape recorders, computers, and long distance telephone communication. Astronauts could never have walked on the moon without thousands of electronic devices, including the computer that safely guides their ship.

Basic Principles of Electronics

All matter is made up of atoms. Each atom consists of one or more electrons in orbit around a small, heavy nucleus made of protons and neutrons. Atoms usually have equal numbers of positively charged protons and negatively charged electrons. Certain materials, called *conductors,* contain free electrons—electrons that are not in orbit around a nucleus. These free electrons can flow along the conductor, producing an electric current. Copper is a good conductor.

However, electric current does not have to flow through a conductor. Electrons flowing through a gas, liquid, or vacuum also form an electric current, and currents formed in this way are the subject of electronics.

Electrons must escape from the atoms they orbit to produce a current outside of a conductor. Electrons can be freed in several ways. (1) A substance can be heated so that its atoms move about rapidly and bump together. This causes some electrons to be knocked out of their orbits. (2) Light striking certain substances can cause atoms to give up electrons. (3) Electrons or other tiny particles can be "shot" at the substance. The electron "bullets" run into the atoms of the substance, knocking many more electrons out of their orbits.

If the electrons are freed in air, they are quickly captured by nearby atoms. This means that no useful electric current is produced. Scientists have developed several ways to overcome this problem.

The Vacuum Tube

Vacuum tubes are called vacuum tubes because almost all the air has been pumped out of them. The most important vacuum tubes were invented in the early 1900s. The simplest one is a *diode.* It has two electrodes, a *filament* or *cathode* that emits (gives off) electrons, and a *cold plate* or *anode* that attracts and

▼*The tiny size of electronic circuits in use today can be seen by comparing the integrated circuits with the coin they partially cover. The surrounding magnified area is an arrangement of individual circuits.*

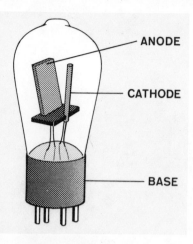

▲ A simple vacuum tube, the diode.

collects electrons. When the anode has a positive charge (when it has many protons and few electrons), the electrons from the filament flow to the anode, because opposite charges attract. When the anode has a negative charge (when it has few protons and many electrons), the electrons from the filament are not collected, because like charges repel. For this reason, diodes are often used to change alternating current (AC) to direct current (DC)—current that flows in only one direction. These special diodes are called *rectifiers,* and your TV set uses several of them.

Another special diode is the *X-ray tube.* When the current to the anode is very strong, electrons are drawn to the plate with great force. When the electrons crash into the anode, they stop suddenly, and X-rays are given off.

CATHODE RAY TUBE. One of the most important special vacuum tubes is the cathode ray tube, or CRT. It produces the picture in your television set. It also is used to provide pictures taken through an electron microscope, and to give a visible pattern of a sound or an electric signal on the screen of an instrument called an *oscilloscope.*

Inside the glass "envelope" of a CRT, the filament (or cathode) produces free electrons. Several special anodes are placed along the tube. The anodes are usually hollow cylinders. Because of their special shape, these anodes do not collect most of the free electrons, as the anode of a diode does. The anodes of a CRT attract electrons, but most of these tiny particles pass through the hollow centers of the anodes. This arrangement of filament and anodes is known as an *electron gun* because it causes electrons to shoot down the tube at very high speeds. The electrons rush down the tube until they crash into the TV screen, which is coated with special fluorescent material. Each electron collision causes a tiny flash of light. Electric and magnetic fields are used to aim the stream of electrons at the right part of the screen, so that the collisions form a picture.

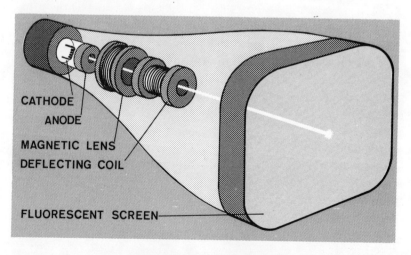

▶ A cathode ray tube.

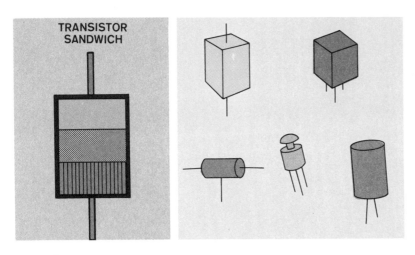

TRANSISTOR SANDWICH

◀ *Transistors are made in many shapes and sizes, but all consist of semiconductor "sandwiches."*

Transistors

Transistors also carry electrical current. They have replaced vacuum tubes in many uses, because transistors can be made much smaller and are not as fragile as vacuum tubes. Can you imagine a "pocket" radio with five or six tubes?

A transistor is made of *semiconductors,* materials, such as silicon, that carry electrical current, but not as well as conductors do. A transistor is a semiconductor "sandwich," one slice of one semiconductor substance between two slices of another semiconductor substance. In one type of transistor, when a weak current flows to the *base,* or middle of the sandwich, a much stronger current flows from one side of the transistor—called the *emitter*—to the other side—called the *collector.* Scientists add tiny amounts of other chemical elements, such as arsenic or phosphorus, to a silicon crystal to control the direction in which the current flows.

Transistors were first produced in 1948. They were first used in a commercial product—hearing aids—in 1952. Transistors have now replaced vacuum tubes in many products (called *solid state* devices) from television sets to computers.

Many other electronics devices are used with vacuum tubes and transistors to produce devices that help people live more pleasant lives. They also help scientists explore the universe.
ALSO READ: ATOM, ELECTRICITY, MAGNET, MASERS AND LASERS, RADIO, TELEVISION, X-RAY.

ELEMENT   Have you ever wondered what things are made of? If you have, you were thinking about a question that puzzled men for thousands of years. Today we know that a few substances, called *elements,* make up all others.

First Ideas

Thales, a wise man of ancient Greece, was the first person to state an idea about the source of elements. He said that everything is made of water. He had seen water as ice, steam, fog, rain, and dew. If water could take all these forms, might it not take the form of any material? Thales thought it could, so he said that water is the element of which everything is made.

But certain Greeks disagreed. One said that air is the only element; another said fire; and still another, earth. One man, Democritus, said that everything is made up of extremely small, hard particles called *atoms*. One of the greatest of Greek wise men, Aristotle, named four elements—water, air, fire, and earth. For the next 2,000 years, people believed that all things were made up of these four "elements."

THE ROAD TO CHEMICAL CHANGES. During the Middle Ages, men in Europe and Asia called *alchemists* spent much time trying to change cheap metals, such as lead, into gold. Their attempts failed, but they learned that certain substances could be changed into more than one material. But some substances, such as gold, silver, lead, copper, tin, antimony, mercury, carbon, and sulfur, could not be divided or broken down. This understanding gave a good definition of what an *element* is— *a substance that cannot be broken down into simpler substances.*

Some substances are easier to break down into elements than others. Ask an adult to help you burn a marshmallow. You cannot see the oxygen and hydrogen that are driven off in the smoke of the fire. But the black material that is left is carbon. The heat of the fire has caused a chemical change.

DALTON'S IDEA. In 1804, an English schoolmaster, John Dalton, revived Democritus's idea that all substances are made up of tiny particles called atoms. Dalton went further. He said that all the atoms of any chemical element are exactly alike, having the same weight, size, and form, and that the atoms of one element are different from those of all other elements. This idea gives us another definition of an element—*a substance made up entirely of atoms of the same kind.*

ATOMIC NUMBERS. Scientists worked out a new idea of an atom soon after the beginning of the twentieth century. Each atom has a central part called a *nucleus*. Around the nucleus move very small particles called *electrons*. Inside the nucleus itself are two kinds of particles, *neutrons* and *protons*. The hydrogen atom, which is the lightest of all atoms, has one proton. Each succeeding heavier atom has one more proton than the atom before it. The number of protons in the nucleus of an atom is called the *atomic number* of that element. Every atom has the same number of protons and electrons, so the atomic number also tells the number of electrons.

Scientists found that the idea of atomic numbers gave a more exact definition of an element—*a substance made up of atoms all having the same atomic number.*

ATOMIC WEIGHT. Chemists have learned that electrons have

▲*Some metallic elements must be extracted from other elements since they rarely occur naturally alone. The gold nuggets* (above) *were obtained by the simple panning method that was once used by prospectors. Mercury* (below) *must be extracted by a heating and condensation process.*▼

CHEMICAL ELEMENTS

ELEMENT	SYMBOL	ATOMIC NUMBER	ATOMIC WEIGHT	DISCOVERER(S)
Actinium	Ac	89	227	Debierne
Aluminum	Al	13	26.98	Oersted
Americium	Am	95	243	Seaborg, James, Morgan, and Ghiorso
Antimony	Sb	51	121.76	Valentine
Argon	Ar	18	39.944	Ramsey and Raleigh
Arsenic	As	33	74.91	Magnus
Astatine	At	85	210	Corson, MacKenzie, and Segré
Barium	Ba	56	137.36	Davy
Berkelium	Bk	97	249	Seaborg, Thompson, and Ghiorso
Beryllium	Be	4	9.013	Vauquelin
Bismuth	Bi	83	209.00	Valentine
Boron	B	5	10.82	Davy
Bromine	Br	35	79.916	Balard
Cadmium	Cd	48	112.41	Stromeyer
Calcium	Ca	20	40.08	Davy
Californium	Cf	98	249	Seaborg, Thompson, Ghiorso, and Street
Carbon	C	6	12.011	Found long ago
Cerium	Ce	58	140.13	Klaproth
Cesium	Cs	55	132.91	Bunsen and Kirchoff
Chlorine	Cl	17	35.457	Scheele
Chromium	Cr	24	52.01	Vauquelin
Cobalt	Co	27	58.94	Brandt
Copper	Cu	29	63.54	Found long ago
Curium	Cm	96	245	Seaborg, James, and Ghiorso
Dysprosium	Dy	66	162.51	Boisbaudran
Einsteinium	E	99	253	Ghiorso
Erbium	Er	68	167.27	Mosander
Europium	Eu	63	152.0	Demarcay
Fermium	Fm	100	254	Ghiorso
Fluorine	F	9	19.00	Scheele
Francium	Fr	87	223.0	Perey
Gadolinium	Gd	64	157.26	Marignac
Gallium	Ga	31	69.72	Boisbaudran
Germanium	Ge	32	72.60	Winkler
Gold	Au	79	197.0	Found long ago
Hafnium	Hf	72	178.50	Coster and Hevesy
Hahnium	Ha	105	262	Ghiorso
Helium	He	2	4.003	Ramsay
Holmium	Ho	67	164.94	Cleve
Hydrogen	H	1	1.0080	Cavendish
Indium	In	49	114.82	Reich and Richter
Iodine	I	53	126.91	Courtois
Iridium	Ir	77	192.2	Tennant
Iron	Fe	26	55.85	Found long ago
Krypton	Kr	36	83.80	Ramsay and Travers
Lanthanum	La	57	138.92	Mosander
Lawrencium	Lw	103	256	Ghiorso, Sikkeland, and Larsh
Lead	Pb	82	207.21	Found long ago
Lithium	Li	3	6.940	Arfvedson
Lutetium	Lu	71	174.99	Welsbach and Urbain
Magnesium	Mg	12	24.32	Liebig and Bussy
Manganese	Mn	25	54.94	Gahn
Mendelevium	Mv	101	256	Ghiorso, Seaborg, Harvey, Choppin, Thompson
Mercury	Hg	80	200.61	Found long ago
Molybdenum	Mo	42	95.95	Hjehn
Neodymium	Nd	60	144.27	Welsbach
Neon	Ne	10	20.183	Ramsay and Travers
Neptunium	Np	93	237	McMillan and Abelson
Nickel	Ni	28	58.71	Cronstedt
Niobium	Nb	41	92.91	Hatchett
Nitrogen	N	7	14.008	Rutherford
Nobelium	No	102	253	Ghiorso
Osmium	Os	76	190.2	Tennant
Oxygen	O	8	15.999	Priestly and Scheele
Palladium	Pd	46	106.4	Wollaston
Phosphorus	P	15	30.975	Brandt
Platinum	Pt	78	195.09	Ulloa
Plutonium	Pu	94	242	Seaborg, McMillan, Wahl, and Kennedy
Polonium	Po	84	210	P. and M. Curie
Potassium	K	19	39.100	Davy
Praseodymium	Pr	59	140.92	Welsbach
Promethium	Pm	61	145	Glendenin and Marinsky
Protactinium	Pa	91	231	Hahn and Meitner
Radium	Ra	88	226.05	P. and M. Curie and Bemont
Radon	Rn	86	222	Dorn
Rhenium	Re	75	186.22	Noddack and Tacke
Rhodium	Rh	45	102.91	Wollaston
Rubidium	Rb	37	85.48	Bunsen and Kirchoff
Ruthenium	Ru	44	101.1	Claus
Rutherfordium	Rt	104	257	Ghiorso
Samarium	Sm	62	150.35	Boisbaudran
Scandium	Sc	21	44.96	Nilson
Selenium	Se	34	78.96	Berzelius
Silicon	Si	14	28.09	Berzelius
Silver	Ag	47	107.880	Found long ago
Sodium	Na	11	22.991	Davy
Strontium	Sr	38	87.63	Crawford
Sulfur	S	16	32.066	Found long ago
Tantalum	Ta	73	180.95	Eckeburg
Technetium	Tc	43	99	Perrier and Segre
Tellurium	Te	52	127.61	Von Riechenstein
Terbium	Tb	65	158.93	Mosander
Thallium	Tl	81	204.39	Crookes
Thorium	Th	90	232.05	Berzelius
Thulium	Tm	69	168.94	Cleve
Tin	Sn	50	118.70	Found long ago
Titanium	Ti	22	47.90	Gregor
Tungsten	W	74	183.86	D'Elhujar
Uranium	U	92	238.07	Klaproth
Vanadium	V	23	50.95	Sefstrom
Xenon	Xe	54	131.30	Ramsay, Travers, Marignac
Ytterbium	Yb	70	173.04	Gadolin
Yttrium	Y	39	88.92	Marggraf
Zinc	Zn	30	65.38	Klaproth
Zirconium	Zr	40	91.22	

almost no weight at all. The weight of an atom is concentrated in its nucleus. Protons all weigh the same, and neutrons all weigh the same. And a neutron weighs as much as a proton. A proton (or neutron) weighs more than 1,800 times as much as an electron.

The weight of an atom (in *atomic mass units*) can be found by adding the number of protons and neutrons in its nucleus. An atom of hydrogen has one proton and no neutrons in its nucleus, so the atom's *atomic weight* is 1. The nucleus of a carbon atom contains six protons and six neutrons. Its atomic weight is 12. A uranium atom has 92 protons and 146 neutrons. What is its atomic weight?

The Periodic Table

In 1869, a Russian chemist, Dmitri Mendeleev, arranged all the elements that were then known into a table according to their increasing atomic weights.

If you were to look up the properties of all the elements, you would find that the elements in each vertical row of the table have similar chemical properties. In the horizontal rows, the properties of the elements repeat themselves in each row. On the left of each row is a light metal, then follow heavier metals, then nonmetals, and finally one or two gases. The fact of this repetition caused Mendeleev to say that the properties of the elements repeat in definite periods as their atomic weights increase. In the modern *periodic table,* elements are listed in order of increasing atomic numbers.

TRANSURANIUM ELEMENTS. Chemists made the first synthetic element, neptunium, in 1940. This was done by bombarding uranium with neutrons. Neptunium has an atomic number of 93, one more proton than uranium. Twelve more synthetic elements have been made since 1940. Because all are heavier than uranium, the new elements are called *transuranium* elements. *Trans* is Latin for "beyond" (or heavier than) uranium. Only very small quantities of transuranium atoms have been made. Chemists and physicists are attempting to produce still more new elements with even higher atomic weights.

CHEMICAL SYMBOLS. So far, scientists have discovered 105 elements. Ninety-two have been discovered in nature, and thirteen have been made in "atom smashers" by chemists and physicists. Of the natural elements, 79 are normally solids, 2 are liquids, and 11 are gases. Sir Humphry Davy, a famous British chemist, discovered six of these elements.

Chemists use special abbreviations, or *symbols,* to name the elements. For instance, instead of writing out "hydrogen," the chemist writes H. The symbol for an element may be the first letter of its name, as N for nitrogen and S for sulfur. But the names of many elements begin with the same letter (11 elements begin with the letter C). So the symbols for most elements are made up of the first letter and one more, as Ca for calcium and Cd for cadmium. The symbols for some of the elements are abbreviations of the Latin names of those elements, for example, Fe for *ferrum,* the Latin word for iron. Symbols used to describe a combination of elements are called a *formula.*

ALSO READ: ATOM, CHEMISTRY, PHYSICS, SCIENCE.

◀*A herd of elephants in a field on the island of Ceylon. Asian elephants are a darker gray than their African cousins.*

ELEPHANT An elephant can uproot a tree or pick a flower without bruising a petal. It thunders through the forest but can balance its fantastic weight on one foot before a circus audience. The elephant is the largest living land mammal, but will respond to the friendship of a small boy.

Ancestors of modern elephants lived on all continents except Australia. Ancient Asians knew the *woolly mammoth.* This hairy beast stood about 10 feet tall and had spiral tusks. The ancestors of American Indians probably knew the *mastodon.* It was about the same size as the woolly mammoth but had straight tusks and less hair. Today, however, only two species of elephants exist—the *Indian* and the larger *African.*

▲*An elephant and her baby cross a road in Africa. Most African elephants have tusks, ears, and a trunk bigger than the Asian elephants have.*

	INDIAN ELEPHANT	AFRICAN ELEPHANT
Height	8 to 10 feet	10 to 14 feet
Weight	about 11,000 pounds	11,000 to 15,000 pounds
Highest point	top of head	shoulder
Length of tusks	4 to 6 feet (female has none or none visible)	up to 11 feet (female's are shorter)
Length of ears	2 feet	up to 5 feet
"Fingers" in trunk	one on bottom of opening	two, one each on top and bottom of opening
Color (when not dusty)	grayish-brown	dark gray or dark brown
Where found	India, Burma, and nearby islands	Africa, south of the Sahara Desert

▲ *An elephant uses its amazing trunk for feeding, as well as for smelling and drinking.*

It might be awkward for you to have a nose that touched the ground. But the elephant finds its trunk, or proboscis, a very handy tool. Nostrils at the end of the trunk are used in breathing. When an elephant walks along the bottom of a river (it can't swim), the tip of the trunk is held above the water. Below the nostrils in the open end of the tube-like trunk is at least one tiny finger-like piece jutting up. The elephant uses the "finger" to pick up small objects. An elephant picks up the masses of plant food it eats in its hollow trunk and then curves the trunk into its mouth, dropping the food down its throat. It drinks water the same way—sucking up 40 gallons daily! Poking out from most elephants' mouths under the trunk are two long tusks. They are enlarged teeth, like the fangs of a cat but much larger. The tusks are used for defense, and, like teeth, they may wear down or be broken off. An elephant's call is a trumpeting sound that echoes through the forest or across the grasslands.

An elephant's massive body is supported by four legs shaped like thick tree trunks. Usually five hoof-like toenails grow on each foot. An elephant's knees are in the middle of the legs like a man's (the knees of most mammals are tucked into the top of the legs where they join the body). But full-grown elephants are so heavy they often prefer not to bend their knees to lie down on the ground and so they sleep standing up.

Elephants are like man in more ways than their knees. They live in groups called herds. They defend a wounded member of the herd. Within the herd, they appear to have rules and customs that govern each member, from the old female leader to the youngest baby. A baby, or calf, drinks its mother's milk for almost a year and stays close to her for five years. Elephants reach adolescence at about age 14 and live to be 65 or 75 years old. And, like man, they lose most of their hair as they grow older.

Elephants have been used by man for almost 4,000 years. First they were killed for their ivory tusks, and the ivory was used to make beautiful carvings and tools. Then they were used like tanks, carrying warriors into the midst of battle. They also served as transportation for kings who rode inside an ornamented chair-like box called a *howdah*. The rare white elephants were highly prized by royalty. Other kings used elephants to pull chariots. Elephants then became "workhorses." In Burma, they have been used for centuries to move heavy logs of teak. And, finally, elephants served double-duty in circuses. At night, they shifted heavy equipment. And by day they delighted audiences with their performances.

Through all these centuries, elephants have never become truly domesticated. They breed in captivity, but elephant handlers prefer to capture fresh elephants instead of breeding them. A female elephant cannot work during the almost two years before her offspring is born. And the young are not strong enough to work until they are about 14. Wild elephants, however, can be trapped fairly easily, and they quickly become tame enough to obey their trainer's commands. Elephants react to directions given by a sharp rod poked into their thick skin. They also respond to spoken orders and seem to learn man's language. Elephants often become very fond of their trainers and may become unhappy if they are replaced. You may have heard the saying that elephants never forget. Like people, they remember those who have been good to them.

ALSO READ: CIRCUS, HANNIBAL, MAMMAL, MAMMALS OF THE PAST.

ELEVATORS AND ESCALATORS Tall buildings, or skyscrapers, stretch upward in every large city. In New York City, giant buildings 80 and 100 stories high look down on buildings only 50 stories high. But look at a picture of New York City in 1850. The buildings were small. Most buildings had only two or three floors. The biggest buildings were only a little higher. Tall buildings were constructed only rarely before the invention of the *elevator.*

Elisha Graves Otis first showed his elevator at the 1854 New York World's Fair. He designed this elevator for freight. It hung from strong ropes. The ropes ran up to a large drum powered by a steam engine. The drum turned one way to lower the elevator. It turned the other way to pull the elevator up. Otis also invented a safety device to stop the elevator from falling if the lift rope broke.

Factories and warehouses soon began installing freight elevators. And in 1857, Otis put his first passenger elevator in a New York City building. It was an immediate success. People no longer had to walk up many steps. Soon buildings began to be built taller. Improved elevators appeared. The first improvement came with the hydraulic elevator in 1871. The elevator car sat on top of a long metal plunger. The plunger went into a cylinder at the bottom. When water was forced in the cylinder, the plunger moved up. When water was released, the plunger moved down. Hydraulic elevators moved more smoothly than the earlier steam-engine elevators. Another type of hydraulic elevator went into the tallest buildings. The elevator car hung from ropes or cables. The cables went through pulleys to a short hydraulic plunger. As the plunger moved in or out, the cables pulled the car up or down.

Modern elevators powered by electric motors began replacing other elevators in the 1890s. Electric elevators hung from long steel cables. Powerful motors pulled the cables swiftly up or down. An elevator operator rode in the car. He controlled the car by a switch that ran the electric motors at the top of the

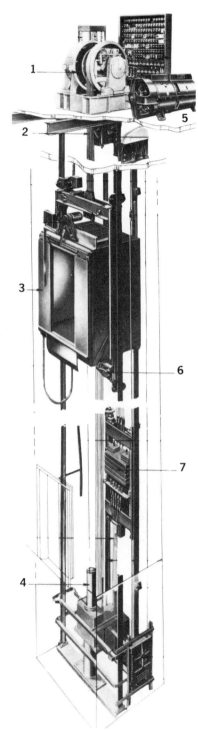

▲ *Major parts of a modern elevator: (1) pulley motor, (2) hoist ropes, (3) passenger car, (4) car buffer, (5) motor generator, (b) safety device, (7) counterweight.*

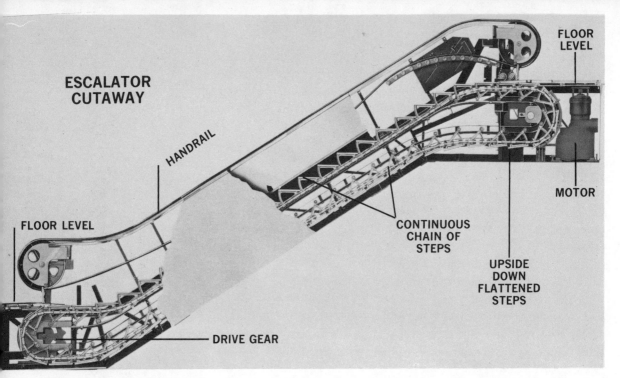

ESCALATOR CUTAWAY

FLOOR LEVEL

HANDRAIL

FLOOR LEVEL

MOTOR

CONTINUOUS CHAIN OF STEPS

UPSIDE DOWN FLATTENED STEPS

DRIVE GEAR

▼*An early hand-operated elevator.*

elevator shaft. In recent years, automatic elevators have replaced elevators with operators. In an automatic elevator, the passenger pushes a button for the floor number he wants. The button is an electric switch that stops the elevator at the right floor. The newest automatic elevator systems have computers to control elevator operation.

Escalators are moving stairs used in stores, railroad and airline terminals, and other places. One of the first escalators was installed at the Paris Exposition of 1900. Escalator steps connect to a chain or belt. The chain travels endlessly around electric-powered gears, or drive shafts. Steps flatten out at the top and bottom of the escalator to line up with a solid platform. Steps on an "up" escalator then curve around and go down.

Escalators move about 90 feet per minute. This is much slower than elevators. Different types of elevators move at different speeds. Some move at 100 feet per minute, but others can travel at speeds up to 1,700 feet per minute. For going up or down only a few floors, escalators are often better.

ALSO READ: ARCHITECTURE.

EL GRECO (about 1541–1614) One of the great artists of Spain was a foreigner with a hard-to-pronounce name, known in Toledo as "the Greek." Today, we remember him, Domenikos Theotocopoulos, by his nickname in Spanish—El Greco.

His early training on the island of Crete as an artist was in the Byzantine style—in the manner of Eastern Orthodox icons. El Greco continued to paint this way, even though he went to Italy to study while in his twenties. He worked under the great artist

Titian in Venice, and then went on to Rome to study the work of the masters Raphael and Michelangelo.

The artist then traveled to Spain, where he settled in the city of Toledo. Over the next 36 years, he painted landscapes, portraits, and many pictures of saints and religious scenes.

The saint pictured here is Saint Martin, dividing his cloak in two to give half to a beggar. According to the legend, the beggar later turned out to be Jesus. Saint Martin wears the dress of a Spanish gentleman of El Greco's time, although the saint actually lived in the 300s. The beggar (the hidden Christ) does not look bent down or defeated. Saint Martin looks sympathetic and concerned about the shivering beggar.

Can you see the Byzantine way of painting? Do you see the lack of depth, or *perspective,* for instance? The artist puts figures up in the foreground in front of a very low horizon. But other features of El Greco's paintings are entirely his own creation. His people have a strange, mystical look, as if from another world. His figures and landscapes are often lengthened and twisted to vividly portray this feeling. His colors combine brilliant splashes of light and somber shadows. And they almost seem to move. To El Greco, movement was all important.

Many of El Greco's works decorated the chapels and monasteries of the city of Toledo. But when he died, El Greco was almost forgotten. His style of painting went out of fashion. French painters 200 years later, particularly Paul Cézanne, rediscovered him. El Greco's paintings from long before expressed feelings in ways that modern artists were trying to achieve in their own work.

ALSO READ: ART HISTORY; BYZANTINE EMPIRE; CEZANNE, PAUL.

▲Saint Martin and the Beggar *by El Greco. National Gallery of Art in Washington, D.C., Widener Collection.*

ELIOT, T. S. (1888-1965) In T. S. Eliot's first important poem, *The Love Song of J. Alfred Prufrock,* many lines describe Prufrock's feelings at a party. Prufrock is sure that everyone is talking about him. Can you understand how he feels?

In *The Waste Land,* a long poem in five parts, Eliot compares the emptiness of modern society with societies of the past. *The Waste Land* became one of the most widely discussed poems of the twentieth century.

Thomas Stearnes Eliot was one of the outstanding writers of the twentieth century. He wrote essays, plays, and poems, but he is most famous for his poetry. Born in St. Louis, Missouri, Eliot went to school in the United States, France, and England. He settled in London in 1914, and in 1927 he became a British citizen. He worked as a bank clerk, teacher, editor, and publisher.

Eliot had very strong opinions about literature, modern life, and religion, and most of his writing expresses his feeling on these subjects. He often wrote about the emptiness of modern

▼*T. S. Eliot, one of the most important poets of the current century.*

life, but his later poems express his feeling that Christianity gave meaning to life and offered hope to mankind. His later poems are very religious in feeling. He was awarded the Nobel Prize for literature in 1948 and the U.S. Presidential Medal for Freedom in 1964.

Two of Eliot's most famous plays are *Murder in the Cathedral* and *The Cocktail Party*. Like all his plays, they are written in unrhymed poetry and deal with religion and morality. Eliot also wrote essays that explained his ideas about literary criticism. He believed that the critic must not let his personal feelings affect his judgment. Eliot was extremely fond of cats and owned many of them. In 1939, he wrote a book of nonsense poetry about cats, *Old Possum's Book of Practical Cats*.

Many poets in this century have broken away from the orderly, rhymed poetic style of the 1800s, but T. S. Eliot was one of the most original. His lines and stanzas are often irregular in length. The rhythms he uses are often unusual, but always powerful. His style has influenced many other modern poets. His plays encouraged the start of poetic drama in English. And his essays have been a major influence on British and American critical writing.

ALSO READ: LITERATURE, NOBEL PRIZE, POETRY.

▲ *Elizabeth I, English queen, who led her country to greatness.*

ELIZABETH I (1533–1603)   Some of the world's greatest rulers have been women, and Elizabeth of England was one of them. She became queen at the age of 25 and ruled for 45 years. She made her country rich. She defeated the Spanish navy and helped to make England a great sea power. She encouraged many great writers, such as Shakespeare and Bacon.

Elizabeth was the daughter of Anne Boleyn, the second of the six wives of King Henry VIII. Her sickly half-brother, Edward, was king for a short time. Then her half-sister, Mary Tudor, was queen. When Mary died, Elizabeth became queen in 1558.

Elizabeth was tall, slim, and had red hair. She was a talented woman who loved fine clothes, jewels, music, and dancing. She picked wise advisers to help her run the country.

While Elizabeth was queen, Sir Francis Drake sailed around the world. His trips, and other trips by English sailors, opened up new markets for English goods. This period of peace and prosperity lasted for many years. But Spain wanted to control the seas. In 1588 Spain sent a huge fleet of over one hundred ships—called the *Armada*—to attack England. Drake, aided by a storm, used smaller, faster ships to defeat the big Spanish ships.

Elizabeth never married. When she was dying, she finally agreed that James VI of Scotland should succeed her. He was the son of Elizabeth's cousin, Mary, Queen of Scots.

ALSO READ: DRAKE, SIR FRANCIS; ENGLISH HISTORY; SPANISH ARMADA.

ELIZABETH II (born 1926) Elizabeth II was crowned Queen of Great Britain in 1952. She is also head of the Commonwealth of Nations (an association of independent nations and territories of the British Empire). Her father was King George VI.

Elizabeth married Prince Philip of Greece on November 20, 1947. He was made Duke of Edinburgh on their wedding day. His wife gave him the title of Prince of the United Kingdom in 1957.

▲*Elizabeth II, present-day English queen.*

Elizabeth does not have any real power as queen. Today, England is run by an elected parliament, which is somewhat like the United States Congress. The queen is a symbol of the British government. Much of her work involves traveling abroad, representing the good will of her country. As head of the British Commonwealth, she particularly visits Commonwealth countries. She also entertains Commonwealth leaders when they visit England. The queen and her husband have visited the United States twice.

Elizabeth has four children, Prince Charles, Prince of Wales and heir to the throne, born in 1948; Princess Anne, born in 1950; Prince Andrew, born in 1960; and Prince Edward, born in 1964. Elizabeth's sister, Princess Margaret, is married to Antony Armstrong-Jones, now known as the Earl of Snowden.

ALSO READ: GEORGE, KINGS OF ENGLAND.

Although Queen Elizabeth's birthday is on April 21, it is officially celebrated in June when the weather is better. She rides side-saddle in a parade and reviews her troops.

EL SALVADOR El Salvador is the smallest country in Central America, but it has more people per square mile than any Central American nation. This little country is tucked in along the Pacific Ocean between Guatemala and Honduras. (See the map with the article on CENTRAL AMERICA.) Most Salvadorians are *mestizos,* people of mixed Spanish and Indian descent. Some are full-blooded Indians.

El Salvador is a country of clear lakes and beautiful beaches. It has a pleasant, mild climate except in the hot, humid, coastal

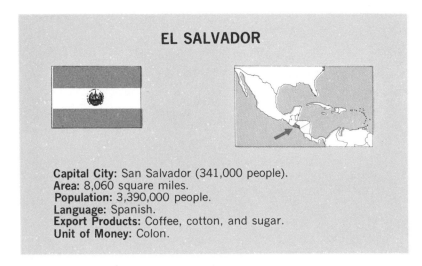

EL SALVADOR

Capital City: San Salvador (341,000 people).
Area: 8,060 square miles.
Population: 3,390,000 people.
Language: Spanish.
Export Products: Coffee, cotton, and sugar.
Unit of Money: Colon.

▶*A view of San Salvador, the capital and largest city in El Salvador. The city is the cultural and commercial center of the country.*

lowlands. Two low volcanic mountain ranges cross the land—one near the coast and the other along the northern border. Between them is an upland of broad basins where the largest cities are found. San Salvador, the capital, has been damaged several times by earthquakes.

Volcanic dust has settled on the valleys and slopes and made very fertile soil. Coffee bushes flourish on the cool hillsides and provide El Salvador's most valuable crop. A few very rich families own most of the coffee *fincas* or plantations.

Many Salvadorians make their living as farmers, raising cotton, beans, corn, rice, sugar cane, and henequen, a plant used for making rope and twine. Some Salvadorians work as farm laborers on coffee plantations. Families are large, and many children work in the fields with their parents. Some Salvadorians work in factories producing cotton textiles, coffee bags made from henequen fibers, and leather goods. El Salvador is the world's main source of balsam gum, which is used for medicinal purposes.

A Spaniard, Pedro de Alvarado, conquered the Indian tribes of El Salvador in the 1520s. El Salvador was a Spanish colony, but broke away from Spain in 1821 along with the rest of Central America. El Salvador has been an independent republic since 1841.

ALSO READ: CENTRAL AMERICA.

ELVES AND FAIRIES   Tales of the "little people," as elves and fairies are often called, are found in the folklore of many lands. They are small, imaginary beings who sometimes help humans. People who believe in them think that elves and fairies can disappear, fly, and change shape.

Elves are imaginary creatures of northern Europe. Good elves are said to be dainty and fair. They play lovely music on golden elfin harps. Like so many of the little people, they dearly love to dance. Other elves are said to be bad. They live underground and keep away from sunlight. They are ugly, brown creatures. *Gnomes, dwarfs,* and *trolls* are usually bad elves.

In England, there is another kind of imaginary elf called a *pixie.* Pixies are attractive little sprites, always dressed in green.

They do many things, mostly mischievous, such as leading travelers astray.

Fairies are charming little people in folk tales. They also love to dance. Fairy rings, or circles of mushrooms, may be seen in forest clearings and in meadows. Where the fairies have danced, no grass grows. It is not wise to disturb a fairy ring, because evil things may happen. If a human being should be so foolish as to actually fall asleep in a fairy ring, he might die, or perhaps be carried off to fairyland, or at the very least be severely pinched. Fairies can be quite helpful when they please. Sometimes, however, fairies are said to leave a *changeling* (an ugly, misshapen dwarf fairy) in the place of a human child.

Another kind of imaginary tiny spirit is the shaggy *brownie* of Scotland. In Germany he is called a *kobold*. Brownies are foot-high household creatures who appreciate a neat, clean house. They will even help wash dishes and sweep floors. Brownies can create much mischief, however. They can make a cow's milk turn sour, a horse go lame, or a milk pail turn over. To keep them happy, it is sensible to put out a bowl of cream and a bit of bread each night. Brownies are extremely fond of cream.

The Irish *leprechaun*, another imaginary creature, looks like a little old man. He stands about two feet tall and wears a tightly laced green coat, knee breeches, and buckled shoes. A leprechaun is highly skilled at making shoes. He is very rich and hides his money in a pot. If you should find a leprechaun, you might be able to persuade him to tell where his pot of gold is hidden. But he will just try to make you look away, and he will disappear.

Writers and musicians have enjoyed writing stories and composing music about elves and fairies. William Shakespeare wrote a play, *A Midsummer Night's Dream.* It is a delightful story about a fairyland kingdom in which Oberon is the king, and Titania is the queen. The brothers Grimm collected folk tales from their native country, Germany. Richard Wagner, a famous German composer, wrote a series of operas based on

◀*A colorful collection of elves and fairies.*

the *Nibelungs,* little creatures in Scandinavian and German mythology.

All of the "little people" are imaginary spirits, of course. But if you wake up in the morning with a strange black and blue mark or a fever blister, or during the day you trip suddenly on some unseen object . . . who knows?

ALSO READ: FABLE; FAIRY TALE; GRIMM BROTHERS; OPERA; SHAKESPEARE, WILLIAM; WAGNER, RICHARD.

▲*President Lincoln reading the first version of the Emancipation Proclamation to his Cabinet on September 22, 1862.*

EMANCIPATION PROCLAMATION President Abraham Lincoln issued the Emancipation Proclamation during the Civil War. It was an important step in freeing the slaves. The proclamation was first announced publicly on September 22, 1862. Lincoln and his cabinet decided it would be a good time to issue the proclamation because the North had just won a victory over the South at the battle of Antietam. Lincoln's proclamation declared that, as of January 1, 1863, slaves "shall be then, thenceforward, and forever free." But the new law applied only to those slaves who were owned in those states that were fighting against the Union. It did not free the slaves in Maryland, Delaware, Kentucky, and Missouri—the slave states that had remained in the Union.

The Confederate States, of course, were not obeying the laws of the Union. So the proclamation had no effect on the slaves living in them. The Emancipation Proclamation did not really free a single slave, but it paved the way for meaningful emancipation laws. The new state of West Virginia abolished slavery that same year, 1863. Maryland and Missouri voted to end slavery in 1864. In 1865, after the Civil War had ended, the Thirteenth Amendment to the Constitution was ratified, making slavery illegal in any part of the United States.

ALSO READ: ABOLITION; CIVIL WAR; LINCOLN, ABRAHAM; NEGRO HISTORY; RECONSTRUCTION; SLAVERY.

EMERSON, RALPH WALDO (1803-1882) The philosophy of Ralph Waldo Emerson expressed many of the finest ideas of early America. He taught that "God is in every man" and in all natural things. He believed that every man should follow his own conscience, even if his ideas did not agree with those of other men or the rules of society. A person could find inner peace and live an honest life only by complete self-reliance. Emerson thought that a person could best experience the presence of God within himself when he was alone and close to nature. He also felt God revealed himself in nature and that man could understand God better by getting closer to nature. He wrote that "In the woods we return to reason and faith."

Emerson was brought up in Boston, Massachusetts. He became a minister of the Unitarian Church. But he found that he could not both follow his own philosophy and obey the rules of the church. He left the church and later settled in Concord, Massachusetts. He wrote down the basic ideas of his philosophy in 1836 in his first book, *Nature*. He also wrote poems and essays, and gave lectures on philosophy. Emerson's ideas inspired many people of his own day. His belief in the individual freedom of all men greatly influenced future American thinkers and writers.

ALSO READ: LITERATURE.

EMOTION   You surely have been angry at someone, and you have been afraid of something. You love some people and hate some. Anger and fear, love and hate are *emotions*. Some other emotions are joy, hope, delight, despair, sadness, and disgust. Everyone has emotions.

▲*Ralph Waldo Emerson, American philosopher.*

Emotions come upon you suddenly. You do not think emotions, you *feel* them. You do not think, "This is an uncaged tiger. I have heard that tigers kill and eat human beings. I am a human being, so I will now be afraid of the tiger." Instead, you feel afraid instantly upon finding yourself near a tiger out of its cage. You do not think afraid, you *feel* afraid.

Emotions can be aroused when information comes to you through your senses. You *see* someone dear to you, and you feel love. You *hear* a scraping sound in a dark room, and you feel fear. You *smell* an unpleasant odor, and you feel disgusted. Emotions can also be aroused by thoughts. You think of someone who embarrassed you, and you feel anger or hate. You think of a test you are not ready to take, and you feel fear or sense defeat.

Thoughts you are not aware of can also bring out emotions. These are called *unconscious* thoughts. For instance, when you were very small, you may have been hurt or embarrassed by an adult with red hair. You forgot about this unpleasant happening, but it is stored in your unconscious memory. You may now dislike people with red hair and not know why. Unconscious thoughts cause the emotion of dislike for redheads.

People seem to be born with a few emotions and gradually learn the rest. A newborn baby fears falling and loud sounds. Yet very young babies do not seem to fear anything else. They must learn to be afraid of fire, dangerous animals, and other things that can harm them. Fear of falling and loud sounds do not have to be learned.

The word "emotion" comes from the Latin word *emovere*, meaning "to move away, or to stir up." Your emotions move you, carry you away, stir you up, cause you to act. Joy may make you jump up and down, clap your hands, dance around, and smile or laugh. Fear may make you run and scream or stand and tremble.

The Empire State Building towers above the New York City skyline.

Emotions also affect your body in ways you are not aware of. Fear causes the adrenal glands to secrete into your blood a chemical substance called *adrenalin.* Adrenalin makes your heart beat faster, your blood pressure rise, and your breathing become faster. It also causes blood to go from your stomach and intestines to your muscles, stopping digestion. Sugar stored in your muscles and liver is sent into your blood. You may tremble and perspire. Your body is ready to react to what is causing your fear. You may run away, or try to fight or hide.

ALSO READ: FREUD, SIGMUND; HORMONE; MENTAL HEALTH; PSYCHOLOGY; SENSE ORGAN.

EMPIRE STATE BUILDING   Have you ever visited a very tall building, or skyscraper, and looked out a window? Cars and houses look very small. Sometimes people become so tiny you can't see them at all. The Empire State Building in New York City, built in 1930, was the world's tallest office building for about 40 years. The structure is made of steel beams riveted together. The 102-story skyscraper was originally 1,250 feet high. A television broadcasting tower, with a beacon on top, was added in 1951, making the Empire State Building 1,472 feet tall. Thousands of visitors come to this skyscraper each year and ride in high-speed elevators to reach the observation decks and view the city. By 1971, even taller skyscrapers were being built in New York and Chicago.

ALSO READ: ARCHITECTURE.

An enameled metal chest made in Limoges, France. Limoges was an important center of the art of enameling for over 400 years, from the 1200s to the 1600s.

ENAMELING   Enameling is an art form in which colored glass is fused (united by melting together) to a metal base. The combination of fused glass and metal is called enamel. The glass used in enameling is not the ordinary kind that cracks as it cools. Enameling glass is a colorless powder, with metallic oxides added for color. Hobbyists today can buy enamel in powdered form in a wide variety of colors.

Enameling is a very ancient craft. Both Chinese and Egyptian art pieces and jewelry can be seen in museums. The Byzantines did beautiful enameling during the tenth and eleventh centuries. Thin strips of metal, including gold, were applied to metal objects. The compartments created by the strips were filled with enamel. This process is called *cloisonné.* St. Mark's Cathedral, in Venice, Italy, has 81 enameled plaques in the altarpiece. French enamel works from Limoges are shown at the Louvre and Cluny museums in Paris and other museums. Benvenuto Cellini's famous enameled chalice is on display at the Metropolitan Museum of Art in New York City.

Hobbyists and artists can make many kinds of enameled objects, such as cuff links, ash trays, bracelets, trays, plates, earrings, necklaces, rings, and plaques. Copper is the most popular metal for this craft. Most of the pre-formed copper shapes are available at arts and crafts supply stores.

Enameling is an "art of fire," so a kiln, or oven, is needed. Art supply stores sell simple, inexpensive kilns, which are small, round electric coil heaters.

To make a simple pendant, first assemble all the things you need before starting.

Pre-formed copper disc with hole near one edge
Bottle of opaque enamel powder
80-mesh strainer, or strainer-top to fit enamel bottle
Clean white paper
Fine emery paper or steel wool
Clean cloth
Asbestos board or brick
Small shovel-shaped spatula, or enameling fork with shield

It would also be a good idea to ask an adult to help you, since you will be using a very hot kiln. Protect the table you're working on with newspapers. Cover the newspapers with a clean white paper. Place the kiln in one corner of the table. Keep handy the spatula or enameling fork and asbestos gloves to protect your hands.

Clean the copper piece thoroughly by dropping it into a bowl containing one cup of vinegar and 1½ tablespoons of salt. Dry and polish the surface of the copper with fine emery paper or steel wool and wipe clean. Using tweezers, place the copper on clean white paper. (Only things with steep walls such as bowls, bracelets, and ash trays must be "painted" with an adhesive so that the enamel will stick to the sides.) Sprinkle the powdered enamel evenly on the copper through a strainer. Try to make a design with the enamel. Place the enameled pendant in the pre-heated kiln, which should be set at 1380 degrees for 2 to 4 minutes. You can peer through the glass top of the kiln and watch the dull powdery surface turn into gleaming, glistening enamel. Carefully remove the finished piece with the spatula and place it on a piece of asbestos to cool.

ALSO READ: HOBBY, JEWELRY, POTTERY AND CHINA.

CLEAN COPPER THOROUGHLY AND DRY WELL

POLISH WITH STEEL WOOL OR EMERY PAPER

PLACE ON WHITE PAPER AND SPRINKLE ENAMEL EVENLY

PUT INTO KILN FOR 2–4 MINUTES SET TEMPERATURE FOR 1380

COOL ON ASBESTOS BOARD

HANDLE COPPER WITH SPATULA

▼*An illustrated page from* Natural History, *an encyclopedia by the Roman scholar Pliny the Elder.*

ENCYCLOPEDIA You are reading an article in an encyclopedia. The word "encyclopedia" comes from Greek words meaning "a circle of learning." A general encyclopedia is a book or a series of books containing the important facts about the most significant people, places, events, and things known to mankind. Other encyclopedias offer more detailed information about special subjects, such as science or music. Some encyclopedias are written especially for children. The information in most encyclopedias is written in the form of articles, which are usually arranged alphabetically.

The oldest encyclopedia that is still in existence was written in the first century A.D. by a Roman scholar named Pliny the

Elder. His encyclopedia, called *Natural History*, has 37 volumes. It covers many subjects, including biology, medicine, art, geography, and agriculture. Pliny spent many years reading books and writing short articles on what he thought was important in each subject. Denis Diderot, a Frenchman, edited a 28-volume encyclopedia between 1751 and 1772. It contained articles on history and science as well as criticism of the way people lived.

Until the 1800s, encyclopedias were written mainly as reference works for scholars. But most modern encyclopedias are designed to offer interesting and useful information to the general reader. Encyclopedias today are written by many authors, who are usually experts on the subject about which they write. Their articles are put together by editors to make attractive books. Most encyclopedias are illustrated with photographs, maps, and diagrams. Encyclopedias are sometimes kept up-to-date by the addition of a new book each year. This "yearbook" has articles about important events from the year before. Some encyclopedias are reprinted often to include new information. One of the oldest and most important encyclopedias of this type is the *Encyclopaedia Britannica*, first published in Edinburgh, Scotland, between 1768 and 1771.

Young Students Encyclopedia

The *Young Students Encyclopedia*, first published in 1972, is intended to inform young people about the world in which they live, and to help them understand man's ideas and language. It has been written to be helpful in school and to be easy to read.

This encyclopedia has more than 2,000 articles arranged in alphabetical order. It has an index, with a guide to the pronunciation of words. The index also lists the birth and death dates of everyone named. Cross-references are included at the end of most articles. These tell the reader which other articles in the encyclopedia offer further information on a particular subject. The encyclopedia has many color photographs to illustrate the articles. The encyclopedia also has maps, tables, and graphs.

The "learning by doing" activities are the most unusual features of this encyclopedia. These are printed in blue in many of the articles. They contain suggestions for ways to use the knowledge in the articles. These suggestions can be fun to follow, but may require the help of an adult.

Other Encyclopedias for Young People

One of the first American encyclopedias for children was the *Book of Knowledge*. It was first published in 1910. The articles in this encyclopedia were not in an alphabetical order. The information was contained in articles on major topics. For instance, a topic such as "animal life" covered a great many ani-

A student researches an assignment with the aid of Funk & Wagnalls New Encyclopedia.

mals in one article. The encyclopedia also had many stories, poems, and games. A *New Book of Knowledge* is now published. It has more short articles, arranged alphabetically. The *Golden Book Encyclopedia* is very simple and useful only for small children. *World Book* is a much more comprehensive encyclopedia that is best for teenagers.

Write down some of the subjects you would like to include if you were to write your own miniature encyclopedia. What title would you pick for your encyclopedia? How would you arrange your subjects? In alphabetical order, as in the *Young Students Encyclopedia*? Perhaps you would want to have an encyclopedia just on animals or sports, or some other special subject you especially like. Would you have separate volumes? How many? Look up the information on your subjects in the *Young Students Encyclopedia.* Try to write in your own words, instead of copying directly from the encyclopedia. Where would you get the pictures you need for your articles? From magazines and newspapers? Photographs that your family has taken? You might like to draw or paint your own pictures. When you finish your encyclopedia, you will want to staple or clip it together, or bind it in folders or notebooks.

ALSO READ: REFERENCE BOOK.

Chinese scholars produced the largest encyclopedia ever written. In the 1600s, more than 2,000 writers worked to put together the *Yung Lo Ta Tien.* This encyclopedia was bound into 11,100 volumes.

ENERGY "I'm so tired. I don't have the energy to do anything!" Have you ever heard anyone say this? What is this "thing" a person needs in order to do *anything?* Energy is the ability to do work. A person must expend (use) energy to throw a ball, ride a bicycle, climb a tree, or even just to breathe. All of these activities are work. Scientists define *work* as "moving against resistance."

Energy must be used to do work. The amount of work done and the energy necessary to do it are both measured by the distance an object moves and the force that must be overcome to keep the object moving. The measuring unit of work and

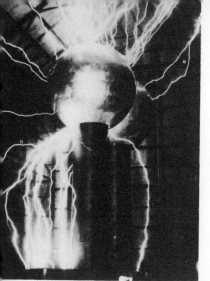

▲ *Potential energy is transformed into kinetic energy in a test on an early Van de Graaff generator.*

energy is the *foot-pound*. If you lift a book that weighs one pound one foot in the air, then you have done one foot-pound of work and expended one foot-pound of energy.

Kinds of Energy

POTENTIAL ENERGY. If you have a rubber band-powered glider, you give it power by turning the propeller, which winds (stretches) the rubber band. As long as you hold the propeller, nothing can happen. But the rubber band is stretched, so it has a *potential* ability to do work. That is, the rubber band may do work in the future. The stretched rubber band has *potential energy*, or energy of position. So does a hammer held high above a nail, or water held by a dam at the top of a hill.

KINETIC ENERGY. Let go of the propeller of your glider. The rubber band now has *kinetic energy*, or energy of motion. It is doing actual work. So is a hammer falling on a nail, or water running downhill and turning a waterwheel. Potential and kinetic energy together are sometimes called *mechanical energy*.

MAGNETIC AND ELECTRIC ENERGY. Magnets can lift iron and steel against the force of gravity. And electricity moving through a coiled wire creates an electromagnet. Because both of these forces can do work, they are both forms of energy.

SOUND AND LIGHT ENERGY. Sound can do work, and so can light. These are two more forms of energy. Light is a part of a very large group of radiations, including X-rays, radio waves, gamma waves, and several more. All of these radiations behave much like light, and together they are called *radiant* energy, much of which comes from the sun.

CHEMICAL ENERGY. The atoms of any chemical compound are normally held in place by certain attractions. Chemical compounds have potential energy, just like a hammer held in the air. If the atoms are freed from their positions—if the attractions are broken—kinetic energy is produced. You can see that chemical energy can be very powerful if you think of a stick of dynamite.

NUCLEAR ENERGY. The nuclei of atoms are made up of tiny particles. The forces that hold these particles together are far stronger than the forces that hold whole atoms in place. When these forces are overcome, an explosion much more violent than that produced by dynamite occurs. Atomic bombs are examples of nuclear energy.

HEAT ENERGY. If you were the pilot of a hot-air balloon, you would build a fire to make your balloon rise, and stop the fire to come back to Earth. You would be using heat energy to fly.

Changing and Measuring Energy

One form of energy can be changed into another form. Chemical energy is changed into light energy and heat energy when wood is burned. In an electric light bulb, electric energy is changed into light energy and heat energy. In a generator, magnetic energy is turned into electric energy. In an electromagnet, electric energy is turned into magnetic energy. In an electric motor, electric energy is turned into mechanical energy.

All other forms of energy can be easily turned into heat, the most basic form of energy. Heat energy is often measured in *calories*. One calorie is the amount of heat needed to raise one gram of water—there are about 28 grams in an ounce—from 14.5 degrees Centigrade to 15.5 degrees. Because any form of energy can be changed into heat, all forms of energy can be measured in calories. The chemical energy of food is frequently measured in calories. A ten-cent bar of milk chocolate, for example, contains about 150 calories.

KINDS OF ENERGY

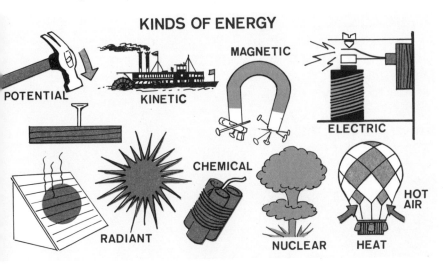

The Conservation of Energy

Energy sometimes seems to vanish. A bouncing ball takes smaller and smaller bounces and finally comes to rest. Has its energy disappeared? No. The energy has changed, however, from kinetic energy to heat. Some of the energy heated the air that the moving ball pushed through. The rest of the energy heated the ground that the ball touched or the ball itself. If you examine every use of energy, you will discover that energy never vanishes.

All energy has a source. To give potential energy to your glider, you must expend chemical energy. To give electrical energy to a flashlight bulb, a battery must use its chemical energy. The bulb then expends the electrical energy to produce light energy.

These facts make up a basic rule, or law of physics—the law of conservation of energy: *Energy may be changed from one form to another, but it can never be created or destroyed.* This is sometimes called the first law of *thermodynamics* (the study of all forms of energy).

This law is true most of the time. But scientists have discovered special situations in which energy can vanish. New matter appears to "replace" the energy. Matter can also vanish, to be replaced by energy. A new law of physics, *The law of conservation of mass-energy,* has been worked out. This law says that the total amount of mass-energy is constant. If one is destroyed, an equivalent amount of the other is created.

Energy is necessary to life. The basic energy of life comes from the heat of the sun. Green plants use this energy. Animals get their energy from eating green plants or from eating other animals that have eaten the plants. Much modern industry depends on potential energy stored millions of years ago in coal, oil, and gas. Man is rapidly using up these energy sources and is hunting for new ones. The lunar rover that astronauts drove around the moon was powered by *solar batteries,* batteries that can change radiant energy directly into electricity. Energy produced by bombarding certain atoms with certain other atoms has given man atomic energy. Scientists are studying other ways to provide energy, too, so that man can continue to live and improve the way he lives.

For further information on:

History, *see* EINSTEIN, ALBERT; GALILEO; NEWTON, SIR ISAAC.

Kinds of Energy, *see* ELECTRICITY, ELECTRIC POWER, HEAT AND COLD, NUCLEAR ENERGY.

Sources and Effects of Energy, *see* ATOM, BATTERY, COAL, ELECTRICITY, ENGINE, EXPLOSIVES, FRICTION, FUEL, GRAVITY AND GRAVITATION, LIGHT, MAGNET, MOTION, MOTOR, PETROLEUM, PHYSICS, PUMP, SIMPLE MACHINE, TURBINE.

ENGINE   Engines are devices that change stored-up (potential) energy into useful mechanical energy. Man has used some kinds of engines—especially windmills and waterwheels—for many hundreds of years. But these engines run out of "fuel" too often. When the air is calm, windmills are useless. When the weather is dry, waterwheels do not turn. Other kinds of engines have been developed because they are more reliable than nature and stronger and faster than man and his animals.

▼*The steam engine invented by Hero. The release of steam made the sphere spin.*

Steam Engines

Steam engines are really very old. The first one known was invented by Hero, a Greek who lived in Egypt nearly 2,000 years ago. You can see his engine in the drawing. It did no work, but it must have been wonderful to watch, because no one—including Hero—understood how it worked. In fact, no one knew for more than 1,500 years how Hero's engine worked.

In 1687 Isaac Newton gave an explanation of how the engine worked. Newton developed three laws (rules) of motion. The

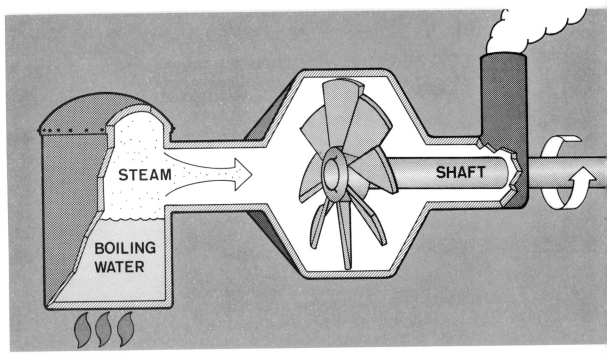

▲ *A steam turbine (external combustion) engine.*

third law says, "For every action there is an equal but opposite reaction." This law sounds complicated, but it is really very simple. You "use" *action-reaction* every time you walk. You push one way on the ground (action), and the ground pushes *you* in the opposite direction (reaction). You move—instead of the ground—because you weigh much less than the Earth. (The Earth really *does* move when you push against it, but it weighs so much that its movement is too small to be measured.) You have seen action-reaction many times. When you jump off the back of a wagon (action), the empty wagon rolls forward (reaction). If you blow up a balloon and let it go, the air shoots out the open end (action), and the balloon shoots around the room until nearly all the air inside the balloon is used up (reaction). You can see that Hero's engine works much like the balloon, and it is called a *reaction* engine. The sphere turned in *reaction* to the *action* of escaping steam.

STEAM TURBINE. Giovanni Branca, an Italian, invented another interesting kind of stream engine in 1629. He used a large wheel divided into blades. Such a wheel is called a *turbine*. As steam from an outside source struck the blades, the large wheel turned smaller wheels.

PISTON ENGINE. A new kind of engine was built by Thomas Newcomen, an Englishman, in the early 1700s. Newcomen's engine had a *piston* (plunger) inside a *cylinder* (tube). One end of the piston was connected to a pump handle in such a way that the weight of the handle pulled the piston to the top of the cylinder. Steam was forced into the cylinder below the rising piston. When the piston reached the top of the cylinder, the steam was shut off, and cold water was shot into the cylinder. The cold water caused the steam to condense (turn back into water). This caused a partial vacuum below the piston. The air pressure above the piston forced the piston down the cylinder, raising the pump handle. Then the cycle would start all over.

Newcomen's engine was slow and used large quantities of steam. James Watt improved the piston engine by designing one in which steam was forced first into one end of the cylinder and then into the other end, moving the piston first one way, then the other. This engine was faster and more efficient than Newcomen's engine.

MODERN STEAM ENGINES AND HOW THEY WORK. Steam engines all depend upon one fact. When a quantity of water is heated and turned into steam, the steam takes up 1,700 times as much room as the water did. If water turns into steam in a closed container (such as a boiler), the water cannot expand, so it produces pressure, or force. In all steam engines, the water is heated in a boiler and then piped to the engine. The fuel is burned outside the engine. For this reason, steam engines are called *external combustion* engines.

Modern steam engines are almost always turbines. A turbine weighs less and runs more smoothly than a piston engine that can do the same work. Steam turbines are often used to power ships and to generate electricity.

Internal Combustion Engines

In an *internal combustion* engine, fuel is burned inside the engine itself. The most common kind of internal combustion engine is the *gasoline piston* engine, which is used to power automobiles. An automobile engine consists of several cylinders arranged in one or two rows. Inside each cylinder is a piston. Also inside each cylinder is a *spark plug,* a device that produces

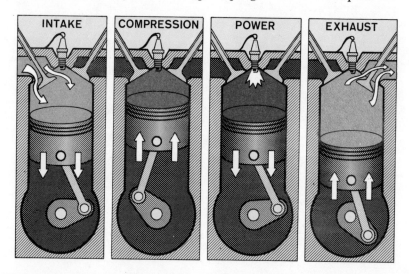

►*A four-stroke internal combustion engine, such as is used in an automobile.*

sparks. A mixture of air and gasoline is forced into the cylinder, and a spark from the spark plug causes an explosion. The explosion gives the piston a mighty push down the cylinder. The pistons of an automobile engine are connected to a rod, called a *crankshaft*. As a piston moves down the cylinder, it causes the crankshaft to turn. When the engine is adjusted so that the cylinders "fire" one after another, the crankshaft is kept turning constantly. The crankshaft is connected to the wheels by a series of gears, so that as it turns, it turns the wheels. In order to clean up our polluted atmosphere, cars will have to use a different kind of engine, or else devices will have to be developed that remove the poisonous gases that these engines now produce.

Small airplanes are usually powered by gasoline piston engines. The crankshaft is connected to the propeller, not the wheels. And the cylinders are most often arranged in a circle, not in straight lines.

One other kind of gasoline piston engine is the *diesel* engine. It has no spark plugs. Instead, it depends upon very hot air to cause the explosions that provide the power.

GAS TURBINE. A gas turbine is much like a steam turbine. But a gas other than steam does the work of turning the wheels, and the fuel is burned inside the engine, rather than outside.

JET AND ROCKET ENGINES. These are action-reaction engines. Hero's steam engine was a peculiar sort of jet, only it depended on external combustion, and modern jet and rocket engines are internal combustion engines. In both jet and rocket engines, hot gases shoot out of the rear of the engine (action), pushing the engine—and the airplane or rocket attached to the engine—forward. The major difference between these two engines is that jets take oxygen from the atmosphere to burn with the fuel, while rocket engines carry an oxygen supply along with them so that they can work outside the atmosphere.

ALSO READ: AUTOMOBILE; DIESEL ENGINE; ENERGY; FUEL; GAS; GASOLINE; HORSEPOWER; JET PROPULSION; MOTOR; NEWTON, SIR ISAAC; TURBINE; VACUUM; WATT, JAMES.

ENGINEERING Have you ever thought of inventing something new and useful? You may have had a good idea, but you lacked the knowledge of how to design, build, and make your invention. Engineering involves all of these steps. Engineers must know how to plan and design structures, machinery, appliances, and many other things. Engineers must know what materials to use and how to put them together. They must also know how to make the things they build with efficiency.

Engineers are sometimes clever detectives. A museum owned a painting that was said to have been made in the fifteenth century. An art expert thought it was a forgery. The museum did not want to scrape paint from the picture for an analysis.

▲*A gasoline piston engine is inspected and tuned before being sent to the assembly area to be put into an automobile.*

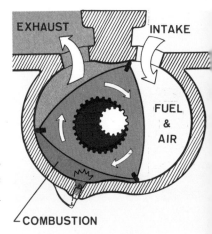

EXHAUST   INTAKE

FUEL & AIR

COMBUSTION

▲*The Wankel, or rotary, engine is a new version of the internal combustion engine. It has no pistons. Instead, a rotating shaft controls the burning of the fuel. Such an engine runs more smoothly and efficiently than an engine with cylinders and pistons.*

▲ *A metallurgical engineer in a steel plant oversees the operation of automatic control equipment.*

A sample had to be obtained without harming the painting.

Two engineers invented a research tool called a *microprobe*. The microprobe is a hollow needle with a diameter 25 times smaller than that of a human hair! The needle was pushed into the painting, making an invisible hole. Then it was pulled out, carrying a core of the paint. Analysis showed that the paint contained titanium oxide. Titanium oxide was not in use before 1920, so the painting could not have been made in the fifteenth century. It was a forgery.

The inventors of the microprobe were *metallurgical* engineers. Metallurgical engineers work in two areas. One area involves ways to get metal from raw ore and to refine the metal. The other area concerns metals after they are refined, and also ways to combine them into alloys. *Metallurgy* is only one of a number of engineering fields open to young men and women.

The oldest engineering profession is that of *civil* engineer. Civil engineers build bridges, tunnels, roads, and buildings. You see examples of their work every day. A special branch of civil engineering is *hydraulic* engineering, which deals with such projects as widening rivers or building canals or dams. *Hydro-electric* engineering involves the use of water for the generating of electricity.

Another civil engineering branch is *sanitary* engineering. Among other things, sanitary engineering is concerned with water and air pollution, food sanitation, sewage treatment and disposal, and pest control. More and more sanitary engineers are needed to deal with these serious problems.

Other engineering specialties are also developing. *Mechanical* engineering, for instance, is primarily concerned with machines, such as automobiles. But mechanical engineering also includes branches dealing with aeronautics, refrigeration, and heating and ventilation, among other fields.

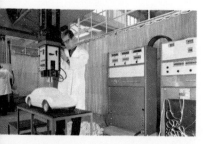

▲ *Mechanical engineers use machines to design, test, and build other machines. Here, a computer is used to record the shape of an automobile.*

Mechanical engineers may work closely with *chemical* engineers. A chemical engineer designs and builds machines that manufacture numerous products, such as toothpaste, medicines, perfumes, plastics, shoes, and cloth.

Another interesting field is that of the *agricultural* engineer. This expert applies general engineering knowledge to large-scale farming operations. For instance, he may be concerned with farm buildings, water supplies, milk coolers, farm machinery, electric power, or heating and ventilation, among other possibilities.

While the agricultural engineer works above ground, another kind of expert, the *mining* engineer, often works deep within the Earth. Mining engineers make surveys, operate drills, and work on various kinds of machines, so they need a working knowledge of mechanical, civil, electrical, metallurgical, and even some chemical engineering.

In our "computer age," a growing field is that of *electrical* and *electronic* engineering. An electrical engineer deals mostly with problems involving wiring and the transmission of electricity over wires. An electronics engineer is concerned with wireless transmissions, such as radio, radar, and television. But these two areas often overlap. The *nuclear* engineer deals with ways to use and control the power contained inside atoms. He often works closely with electronic engineers.

A comparatively new field is that of *oceanographic* engineering, which deals with studies of the oceans and ocean floors. This specialty really requires a knowledge of civil, mechanical, geological, electrical, mining, and other engineering fields.

Even newer than oceanography is *cryogenic* engineering, which involves working with materials, processes, and equipment used at temperatures as low as 456 degrees below zero. This intense cold is attained by the use of liquid oxygen, nitrogen, and other gases, all of which are so cold that ordinary ice is hot by comparison. Cryogenic engineering is important in space exploration.

If you enjoy taking things apart—and putting them together—to find out how they work, and if you enjoy science and arithmetic in school, you may someday want to be an engineer.

ALSO READ: CAREER, ENGINE, INDUSTRIAL ARTS.

▲ *A wind tunnel, designed by an aerospace engineer, is used to test how well a motorcycle can run in strong winds.*

ENGLAND "This royal throne of kings, this sceptered isle . . . This precious stone set in the silver sea . . . This blessed plot, this earth, this realm, this England." So did William Shakespeare describe England in his play *King Richard II.*

England is the largest of the four once-separate countries that make up the United Kingdom of Great Britain and Northern Ireland. Northern Ireland, Scotland, and Wales are the other countries. (See the map with the article on BRITISH ISLES.)

London is the capital of the United Kingdom and its largest city. England is bordered by water on the east and south, and borders on Scotland to the north and Wales to the west. The highest land is in the west. The mountains called the Pennine Chain begin at the border of Scotland and run through central England. In the middle of the country are the rolling hills and valleys called the Midlands. The land is flat and low in the east. The southern part of the country is well-known for beach areas and popular seaside resorts.

Although England is farther north than the northeastern United States, its climate is mild and rainy. In winter, temperatures usually stay above 20 degrees, and in summer below 80 degrees. An ocean current that flows up from the equator passes the coast of England. Winds blowing southwest across this current bring warm air to England in the winter.

England has few natural resources except coal and iron ore.

▲*Newcastle-upon-Tyne in northeastern England is the center of an important industrial area called Tyneside, named after the Tyne River. Shipbuilding and the export of coal are its leading activities.*

▼*An old English cottage in a pastoral setting in Somerset, a beautiful county of deep green rolling farmland in southwestern England. Somerset is world-famous for its cheddar cheese.*

It is a trading country, preparing goods for sale in other countries. England has been successful as a trading country because it has a good transportation system, an excellent merchant marine, good seaports, and is close to the European mainland. England is also one of the world's leading industrial nations. The Industrial Revolution started in English textile factories in the 1700s. Steel production is the most important industry. Textiles, automobiles, ships, and chemicals are other important manufactured products.

About four-fifths of England's land is used for farming. England still must import about half of its food. The land is farmed more intensely than in the U.S., but English farms are generally smaller than American farms. A large part of the land is used for the grazing of beef and dairy cattle and sheep. The main crops are grains, potatoes, vegetables, and fruits.

The names "England" and "English" come from an early tribe, the Angles, who conquered part of the land in the late fifth century. The English language comes from many sources. These include Latin, brought to England by the Romans, and Norman French, brought in 1066 by the followers of William the Conqueror from Normandy. Many English words are spelled slightly differently from the way they are in the United States, such as "colour" instead of "color."

Soccer is the most popular sport in England. Soccer is also called "football," although it is not the same game as American football. Crowds of 100,000 may turn out for important soccer matches. Cricket and rugby are also popular in England, and badminton was developed there.

Traditions are a very important part of English living. The royal family still holds a place in the nation's government, which is a constitutional monarchy. Kings and queens once ruled England with a strong hand. But the Parliament and the people have taken away many powers that once belonged to royalty. Today, the English monarch is more of an adviser to Parliament.

ALSO READ: BRITISH ISLES, ENGLISH CHANNEL, ENGLISH HISTORY, ENGLISH LANGUAGE, INDUSTRIAL REVOLUTION, LONDON, NORTHERN IRELAND, SCOTLAND, UNITED KINGDOM, WALES.

ENGLISH CHANNEL The British people call the narrow stretch of water between England and France the English Channel. Because of its shape, the French call it *La Manche* ("The Sleeve"). The channel has played an important part in English history for thousands of years. Today, it is still a busy waterway. (See the map with the article on BRITISH ISLES.)

The English Channel is 150 miles wide at the western end, where it meets the Atlantic Ocean. It narrows to 21 miles at the eastern end. Here it runs into the Strait of Dover, which links it

◀A view of Creux Harbour on Sark, one of a chain of islands located in the English Channel.

with the North Sea. Resorts and busy seaports line the French and English coasts. The tides in the channel are very strong. The weather is frequently stormy. Fogs sometimes blanket the channel for days. Lighthouses help ships' captains to navigate the waters.

Since early times, invaders from continental Europe have chosen the channel as the best way to reach the English coast. Warships carried the armies of Julius Caesar to Britain in 54 B.C. Thus began more than four centuries of Roman occupation. The last invading army crossed from Normandy in 1066, led by William the Conqueror. The famous defeat of the Spanish Armada in 1588 took place in the area of the English Channel. During World War II, Allied forces crossed the channel in airplanes and ships to begin the offensive that swept across France, into Germany, and ended the war.

Ferries cross the channel regularly. Ideas for building a cross-channel tunnel are being considered. For many years, daring people have tried unusual ways of crossing the English Channel. Many hundreds of swimmers have tried to swim across the 21-mile gap between Dover, England, and Calais, France. Only about 200 have made it. A diver even tried to walk across the bottom of the English Channel, but he gave up part of the way across.

ALSO READ: BRITISH ISLES, FRANCE.

ENGLISH HISTORY   The first people in England came from Europe. They were hunters who used stones to make tools and weapons. People later learned how to use bronze and till the soil. These Bronze Age people worshiped the sun. They moved stones from great distances and put them into big circles, probably to form a place to worship. One of these circles, Stonehenge, is still standing in southern England. The arrangement of the stones indicates that Stonehenge was also a kind of giant calendar. The builders must have had a good knowledge of astronomy.

A tribe, known as the Celts, invaded England between the sixth and the first centuries B.C. They made tools from iron, and they worked as farmers, cattle herders, and traders.

The Romans successfully invaded England in 55 B.C., and ruled it for over 400 years. They built many long roads, as well

▶Hadrian's Wall was a defensive barrier built in northern England about 120 A.D. by the Roman Emperor Hadrian. Parts of the wall still stand and are wide enough to walk on.

as cities, such as York and London. Some groups of people living in England were hostile. One group was the Picts who lived in the northern part of the country. In the 120s, the Romans built an east-west wall across the island, known as Hadrian's Wall, to keep them away. The Romans gradually left the island after 100, because they were needed to protect other territories.

Even before the Romans left England, many tribes began to invade the island. The Angles, the Saxons, and the Jutes came from areas that are now southern Denmark and Germany. These people became known as *Anglo-Saxons.* They brought their families and settled in villages. Many of these villages still exist. The Anglo-Saxons were not the only people to invade England. The Norseman and the Danes first came in the eighth century. The Danes later gained control of much of the land.

Middle Ages

THE NORMANS RULE. The Normans, the last invaders, sailed to England from northern France in 1066. Led by William the Conqueror, they defeated the English king, Harold, at the Battle of Hastings. William became King William I, and he united England into one country. The Normans set up a *feudal system.* The king owned all the land and gave large grants to a few people, called *nobles* or *barons.* In return for the land, the barons and nobles lent troops to the kings to protect them and fight battles. The feudal system lasted for about 200 years.

GOVERNMENT CHANGES. The problem with the feudal system was that the country was not firmly united. The barons often fought with the king and among themselves. Several of them felt a better way to rule the country must exist and began to create the modern English government during the reign of King John I (1199–1216). King John I tried to make the nobles pay high taxes. The barons rebelled, and they forced John to sign a document called *Magna Carta,* or Great Charter, in 1215. It said that the king must, like any other citizen, obey the law. Magna Carta also limited the king's power and guaranteed that no Englishman could be put in prison without a trial. It also provided for the establishment of law courts.

After King John died, the barons and the kings who followed him continued to struggle for power. Gradually, a new type of government developed. The *Great Council,* established in the thirteenth century, was an early form of Parliament.

After Edward III (1312–1377) became king, he wanted to rule greater territory. When he found that he could not rule Scotland, he tried to control France. The *Hundred Years' War* broke out and lasted on and off, between 1337 and 1453.

Shortly after the Hundred Years' War ended, the English went to war again. The new war was between two families. Each family wanted its leader to be king. One family, the House of Lancaster, used a red rose as a symbol. The other family, the House of York, used a white rose as its emblem. The battles these two families fought thus became known as the *Wars of the Roses* (1455–1485). These wars ended when Henry Tudor, a Lancastrian, defeated and killed King Richard III. Henry Tudor was then crowned Henry VII. England was peaceful again.

▲*The English siege of Orléans in 1428 during the Hundred Years' War between England and France. Joan of Arc led the French to victory over the English.*

England Builds an Empire

HENRY VIII FOUNDS THE PROTESTANT CHURCH. Most Englishmen were Roman Catholics when Henry VIII came to the throne in 1509. Henry VIII became angry when the pope refused to let him divorce the first of his six wives. He decided to form his own church. He announced that the king, and not the pope, would be the head of the Church of England. Under Elizabeth I, Henry's daughter, England became a world power. English ships sailed to all parts of the globe to explore and trade. The English navy defeated the Spanish Armada, a mighty fleet of warships, in 1588. The defeat of Spain gave England greater power. Colonization was begun in Virginia.

James Stuart, king of Scotland, followed Elizabeth to the throne. He became King James I of England. He was also James VI of Scotland. So the two countries were united under one king for the first time. James and his son, Charles I, were not very popular. They believed that their right to rule was given to them by God. Many Englishmen did not agree with this "divine right of kings." Moreover, they were unhappy about certain aspects of the church. This group became known as the *Puritans,* or *Roundheads.* Those people who supported the king and his church were called the *Cavaliers.*

Civil war began in 1642, and the Puritans beheaded the king in 1649. The Puritans, led by Oliver Cromwell, controlled the country. After Cromwell's death, people became tired of the rule of the Puritans. Cromwell's son tried to carry on after his father, but he was overthrown. Charles II was then put on the throne. After Charles's death, James II became king. He was

▲*A galleon of the English navy that sailed the seas during the time of Henry VIII. Henry's reign marked the beginning of England's rise as a great sea power.*

►*Charles I visiting his children shortly before his execution by the Roundheads.*

▲*The coronation of Queen Victoria in Westminster Abbey in 1837. Victoria ruled until 1901, the longest reigning English monarch.*

unpopular because he was Roman Catholic. The so-called "bloodless revolution" took place, and Mary, James II's daughter, and her Dutch husband, William, came to the throne as joint rulers. Before they were crowned, Parliament made the king and queen sign a bill of rights. The document limited the rulers' powers over taxation and control over the military.

The *Act of Union,* in 1707, made England, Scotland, and Wales one kingdom, called the United Kingdom of Great Britain. English territory and power expanded rapidly around the world. The only setback in this expansion was the *American Revolution,* after which England lost her American colonies by a treaty signed in 1783. England still held a huge amount of land in North America, later known as Canada. In the next 100 years England spread its empire through Africa and Asia. During the long reign of Queen Victoria (1837–1901), England was the most powerful nation in the world. It was said that the sun never set on the British Empire, because it had spread to all parts of the globe. During this period, England became one of the most important industrial and trading countries in the world.

THE EMPIRE IN TROUBLE. In the early 1900s, trouble started for the empire. Germany had been building up its own empire and a huge army. This led to World War I. England, France, and Russia declared war on Germany and her allies in 1914. The United States entered the war in 1917 on England's side, and Germany was defeated the following year. The war was extremely costly to England, not only in money, but also in people's lives. Hundreds of thousands of English were killed in the fighting.

Meanwhile, many of the Irish wanted to be free from English rule. Finally, in 1921, much of Ireland became independent, except for six counties in the north that stayed with England. Germany had formed another powerful armed force in 1939 and again wanted to become the leading nation in the world. Its army invaded Poland that year. This led to World War II. Much of Europe was invaded and lay in ruins, while parts of England were destroyed. England and her allies finally defeated

THE KINGS AND QUEENS OF ENGLAND

THE ANGLO-SAXONS

Egbert	828–839
Ethelwulf	839–858
Ethelbald	858–860
Ethelbert	860–866
Ethelred I	866–871
Alfred (the Great)	871–899
Edward (the Elder)	899–924
Athelstan	924–939
Edmund I	939–946
Edred	946–955
Edwy	955–959
Edgar (the Peaceful)	959–975
Edward (the Martyr)	975–978
Ethelred II (the Unready)	978–1016
Edmund II (Ironside)	1016–1017

THE DANES

Canute	1017–1035
Harold I (Harefoot)	1035–1040
Harthacanute	1040–1042

THE SAXONS

Edward (the Confessor)	1042–1066
Harold II	1066

THE NORMANS

William I (the Conqueror)	1066–1087
William II (Rufus)	1087–1100
Henry I (Beauclerc)	1100–1135
Stephen	1135–1154

THE PLANTAGENETS

Henry II	1154–1189
Richard I (the Lionhearted)	1189–1199
John	1199–1216
Henry III	1216–1272
Edward I	1272–1307
Edward II	1307–1327
Edward III	1327–1377
Richard II	1377–1399

THE HOUSE OF LANCASTER

Henry IV	1399–1413
Henry V	1413–1422
Henry VI	1422–1461

THE HOUSE OF YORK

Edward IV	1461–1470

RETURN OF THE HOUSE OF LANCASTER

Henry VI	1470–1471

RETURN OF THE HOUSE OF YORK

Edward IV	1471–1483
Edward V	1483
Richard III	1483–1485

THE HOUSE OF TUDOR

Henry VII	1485–1509
Henry VIII	1509–1547
Edward VI	1547–1553
Mary I (Bloody Mary)	1553–1558
Elizabeth I	1558–1603

THE HOUSE OF STUART

James I	1603–1625
Charles I	1625–1649

THE ENGLISH REPUBLIC

Oliver Cromwell	1649–1658
Richard Cromwell	1658–1659

RETURN OF THE HOUSE OF STUART

Charles II	1660–1685
James II	1685–1688
William III (of Orange) His wife Mary II ruled jointly with him until 1694	1689–1702
Anne	1702–1714*

THE HOUSE OF HANOVER

George I	1714–1727
George II	1727–1760
George III	1760–1820
George IV	1820–1830
William IV	1830–1837

THE HOUSE OF SAXE-COBURG-GOTHA

(In 1917, this German family name was changed to Windsor, the name of the royal residence near London).

Victoria	1837–1901
Edward VII	1901–1910
George V	1910–1936
Edward VIII	1936
George VI	1936–1952
Elizabeth II	1952–

*In 1707, the Act of Union was passed by the parliaments of England and Scotland creating the kingdom of Great Britain.

Germany and her allies, Japan and Italy. Again the war was costly to England in money and lives. In many ways the nation has never completely recovered.

BRITISH COMMONWEALTH IS LIKE A BIG CLUB. After World War II England's British Empire began to break up rapidly. England did not want to hold on to this empire by force, so the Commonwealth of Nations was formed. Member countries are independent, but they work together in matters of trade and defense. One former English colony, India, became a republic in 1947. It stayed in the Commonwealth, however. South Africa and many other colonies in Africa, and also Ceylon and Burma, became independent countries. England today is no longer a world power, but it is still a world leader.

For further information on:

Art and Architecture, *see* BIG BEN; CATHEDRAL; CONSTABLE, JOHN; REYNOLDS, JOSHUA; STONEHENGE; TOWER OF LONDON; WESTMINSTER ABBEY.

Explorers and Exploration, *see* COOK, CAPTAIN JAMES; DRAKE, SIR FRANCIS; EAST INDIA COMPANY; EXPLORATION; HUDSON'S BAY COMPANY; RALEIGH, SIR WALTER.

Geography, *see* BRITISH ISLES, ENGLAND, ENGLISH CHANNEL, IRELAND, ISLAND, LONDON, NORTHERN IRELAND, RIVER, SCOTLAND, THAMES RIVER, WALES.

Government, *see* CHURCH AND STATE, COMMONWEALTH OF NATIONS, KNIGHTHOOD, PARLIAMENT, PRIME MINISTER, UNITED KINGDOM, SCOTLAND YARD.

History, *see* AMERICAN COLONIES, AMERICAN REVOLUTION, BOER WAR, CANADA, COLONY, DECLARATION OF INDEPENDENCE, FEUDALISM, HUNDRED YEARS' WAR, INDUSTRIAL REVOLUTION, MAGNA CARTA, WARS OF THE ROSES, WATERLOO, WORLD WAR I, WORLD WAR II.

Important People, *see* CHURCHILL, WINSTON; CROMWELL, OLIVER; ELEANOR OF AQUITAINE; FAWKES, GUY; GREY, LADY JANE; MORE, SIR THOMAS; NELSON, HORATIO; PATRICK, SAINT; PHILIP, PRINCE; WELLINGTON, DUKE OF.

Kings and Queens, *see* ALFRED THE GREAT; ARTHUR, KING; EDWARD THE CONFESSOR; EDWARD, KINGS OF ENGLAND; ELIZABETH I; ELIZABETH II; GEORGE, KINGS OF ENGLAND; HENRY, KINGS OF ENGLAND; JAMES, KINGS OF ENGLAND; JOHN, KING OF ENGLAND; MARY, QUEEN OF SCOTS; MARY, QUEENS OF ENGLAND; RICHARD, KINGS OF ENGLAND; VICTORIA, QUEEN OF ENGLAND; WILLIAM AND MARY.

ENGLISH LANGUAGE When speaking English, do you realize you are saying words from other languages, too? Many of the more than 500,000 words in the English language have been borrowed or adapted from other languages. American Indian, Arabic, Dutch, French, German, Greek, Hebrew, Italian, Latin, Russian, Scandinavian, and Spanish words are used. Big dictionaries not only list the words in the English language and their meanings, but they also give the original *sources,* or beginnings, of the words.

English has grown by many thousands of new words since its beginnings centuries ago. The forms and spellings and pronunciations of these words have changed greatly. Most changes in language take place so slowly that it is very hard to notice they are happening. But if you look backward in history from the twentieth century, you can recognize these changes more easily.

The development of the English language can be divided into three periods—Old English, Middle English, and Modern English. These periods overlap, or blend from one to another. People did not stop speaking or writing a certain way one day and begin to speak or write another way the next. (1) Old English (*OE*)—also called Anglo-Saxon (*AS*)—was spoken from about 450 A.D. to 1100 A.D.; (2) Middle English (*ME*) was spoken from about 1100 to 1450; and (3) Modern English (*E*) has been spoken since about 1450. Changes in the English language occurred in vocabulary, pronunciation, and *inflection*. (An inflection is a change in a word—usually in the final syllable—that shows the word's use within a sentence.)

Early History

The first people to speak some form of the English language lived in present-day Great Britain. These people spoke some version, or *dialect,* of the Celtic language before 450 A.D. One form of Celtic is still spoken in Wales. Britain had been conquered a few hundred years earlier by the Romans, who spoke Latin. The Roman soldiers marched back to Rome to help defend it from attackers after 400. Within the next century, the Britons were overcome by various tribes that came from the region we know as Germany. These Germanic tribes were the Angles, the Saxons, the Jutes, and the Frisians—all of whom spoke similar languages. The Britons' homeland came to be called *England* after the tribe of Angles. The language that slowly developed came to be known as *English,* or *Anglo-Saxon.*

OLD ENGLISH. The oldest form of the English language (OE) was based on the Germanic languages of those tribes that had conquered the Britons. A few Celtic words and many Latin words were kept, mostly military and commercial ones used by the Romans during their long occupation of the country. Other Latin words crept into the language later. Many of these words were religious terms used by missionaries who brought Christianity to England. Other new words and word forms were introduced by the Danes and the Norwegians, who invaded England from Scandinavia during the 800s. Examine the lines from the long Old English poem *Beowulf.*

> Đe ā wæs wundor micel/Đæt sē wīnsele.
> Widæfde heaðodērum,/Đæ hē on hrūsan ne fēal,
> Fæger foldbold, . . .

Translation:
> It was a marvel that the wine-hall withstood the battlers,
> that it did not fall to the ground, beautiful building; . . .

MIDDLE ENGLISH. The Norman Conquest of England in 1066 influenced the English language greatly. Since the Normans

▶ *An example of old English—a hymn written by Caedmon, a poet of the 600s. The picture shows a scene from the Bible.*

came from France, French became the language used by the English ruling class and for much written literature. Latin remained the language of the church, and English continued to be used by the common people.

This was the period of Middle English. The language absorbed some French words directly from the Norman. But since French was based on Latin, most Middle English words had Latin origins or beginnings. Because Latin itself had borrowed many words from Greek, English by this time had traces of Celtic, the Germanic tongues, Latin, Greek, Scandinavian, and French! It was, however, a language by itself because it had developed its own inflections, vocabulary, and pronunciations.

English had become the principal language of the ruling class in England and also of English writers by the mid-1300s. It replaced French in the English law courts and in Parliament (whose members formed the government which advised the English king). But the word *Parliament* itself was not changed. (It came from the French word *parler,* meaning *to speak.*)

Eventually Middle English developed into Modern English. Most of the old inflections were dropped. English began to depend for meaning on the *order* in which words appeared in a sentence, rather than on the changeable *endings* of words. Examine the lines from a poem, "The Whale's Nature," shown below. How is the language different from that in *Beowulf?*

	Translation:
Cathēgrande is a fis	The great whale is a fish
Đe mǫste đat in water is;	The most that in the water is
Đat tū wuldis sieien gēt,	That you would yet say,
Gef đu it sǫg wan it flēt,	If you saw it when it floated,
Đat it wēre an eilǫnd.	That it was an island.
Đat sēte on dē sęsǫnd.	That sat on the sea sand.

MODERN ENGLISH. English is spoken by nearly 400 million people in the world. English is the *native language* (language of their country) of about 300 million of those people. They include Americans, Australians, Canadians, the people of Great Britain, the Irish, New Zealanders, and many South Africans. People who learn English as a second language find it easy in some ways and hard in others. It is easy because, by now, it has very few inflections. English is easy also because it makes new words by joining two old ones together: base + ball = baseball. Something else that makes English easy to learn: new words can be made by just adding beginnings and/or endings to existing words. These beginnings and endings are called *prefixes* and *suffixes.* Here are a few examples.

Prefix	*Word*	*Suffix*
	content	ment
	use	ful
over	board	
un	done	

Some things about the English language, however, make it difficult to learn. The spelling of a word does not always agree with its pronunciation. Pronounce these six words:

true who shoe

blew zoo through

There are six different ways of spelling the same sound!

But other words are spelled the same way and have different meanings. Look up these three words in the dictionary to see how their meanings differ:

well interest pen

Listen to how you pronounce "Mary," "marry," and "merry." Most Americans think that these three words are *homonyms,* words that sound the same but have different meanings. British people, however, pronounce each of these words differently.

The British writer George Bernard Shaw claimed that, according to pronunciation rules of English, "ghoti" could be pronounced "fish." Sound *gh* as in "rough," *o* as in "women," and *ti* as in "nation," and you will see what he meant.

However, many words are pronounced the same way but have different spellings and meanings. Do you know the different meanings of the words listed below?

> capital, capitol
> principal, principle
> fair, fare
> right, write

Idioms also create problems. An idiom is an expression that means something only in its original language. It sounds foolish or unclear when translated word-for-word into another language. One must learn the meaning of the whole idiom, not just the meaning of each word. "Get nowhere," "aim to prove," and "for many a year" are examples of idioms.

As the peoples of the world are drawn closer together because of world trade, easier travel, and new ways of communication, our growing language continues to borrow from other languages.

Here are a few words that have come into the English language from other sources:

English Word	Source
alphabet	Greek (*alphabētos*)
boom	Dutch
dental	Latin (*dentalis*)
hallelujah	Hebrew
lake	French (*lac*)
patio	Spanish
piano	Italian
school	from Old English *scōl*, from Middle English *scole*, from Latin *schola*, from Greek *scholē*
their	Old Norse (theirra)
waltz	German (walzer)

Now, make a list of words you use often, and look them up in a big dictionary to see where they came from!

American English

We usually think of English as being one language. But since the early days when our country was settled by Englishmen, some noticeable differences have developed between British and American use of the language. These differences in spelling, vocabulary, pronunciation, and *dialect* (regional ways of speaking) have resulted in a variation called *American English*.

Noah Webster, a young American schoolteacher, thought that common sense and convenience should determine how words are spelled. He tried to simplify the spelling of a number of English words when he was preparing the *American Spelling Book* (1783) and the *American Dictionary of the English Lan-*

guage (1823). Today, some American words are spelled more simply than the British version.

British	American
checque	check
humour	humor
programme	program
waggon	wagon

Even greater differences in vocabulary exist. Compare these American English and British English words.

British	American
lift	elevator
petrol	gasoline
biscuit	cookie
chemist	druggist
underground	subway

American English has also invented new words by combining two complete words or parts of them. For example:

countdown
hang-up
motel (motor hotel)
sportscaster (sports broadcaster)

Pronunciation differences are also easily noticed. Englishmen *elide* (run together) syllables, as in Worcestershire (WUS-ter-sher). There are also differences in the use of vowel sounds and emphasis on syllables.

Every language has its own dialects or varieties spoken by people of certain groups or regions. "New England," "Southern," and "Standard American" are the three main dialects of American English. Although differences are easy to hear, speakers of each of the dialects can understand one another. "Standard American" is most commonly spoken and is the model for radio and television speakers.

For further information on:

Origin of Language, *see* CHINESE, GERMAN LANGUAGE, GREEK, LANGUAGES, LATIN, ROMANCE LANGUAGES, RUSSIAN, SCANDINAVIAN LANGUAGES, SPEECH.

Use of Language, *see* FIGURES OF SPEECH, GRAMMAR, LANGUAGE ARTS, PARTS OF SPEECH, PRONUNCIATION.

Written Language, *see* ALPHABET, PICTURE WRITING, WRITTEN LANGUAGE.

ENGRAVING see ETCHING AND ENGRAVING.

ENZYME Enzymes are substances produced by living organisms that make possible the process of breaking down and building up of materials in the body. Enzymes are all catalysts. A *catalyst* is a chemical that causes or speeds up a chemical reaction, but which is not itself used up in the reaction. You can see in the drawing how enzymes work to take apart and build substances.

Without enzymes to work on the chemicals that make up our cells, life as we know it would be impossible. Enzymes enable the simplest virus to enter cells in order to reproduce itself. At the other end of the scale, a complex biochemical organism such as man could not function without enzymes. Enzymes are involved in every aspect of our body functions.

Enzymes are produced within living cells, and that is where most of them do their work. Digestive enzymes are one exception. They work outside the cells, where they break down the food we eat into a form that can be absorbed by the body. Blood clotting is caused by another enzyme that operates outside of the cells where it is produced.

A very large number of chemical reactions are always in progress inside any living thing. Injured tissue must be healed. Worn-out cells must be replaced. Food must be used to provide energy. And such processes must always be carefully controlled so that they do not get out of hand. All of these activities are controlled by enzymes. Enzymes start a process, other enzymes stop it, and still other enzymes continue it once more. Throughout a person's life, his body is controlled by the activities of enzymes. Without enzymes, none of the processes that are called *metabolism,* the chemical activities of the body, could take place.

An enzyme works by acting on a particular substance, combining with it, and changing it chemically. The enzyme is then released and is ready to go through the same process again.

Most enzymes act on only one kind of *substrate,* or substance. Each enzyme does very specialized work. So a large number of enzymes is necessary to control the many different reactions involved in metabolism.

Enzymes in a system often work together as a group. One enzyme acts on a substrate. When it has done its work another enzyme goes to work, then another and another. The whole process is rather like a chain of dominoes falling over. The last domino—or enzyme—cannot work until the next-to-last domino —or enzyme—has done its part, and so on, all the way back to the first part of the chain.

ALSO READ: BIOCHEMISTRY, DIGESTION, METABOLISM.

EPSTEIN, SIR JACOB (1880–1959) Jacob Epstein's sculpture once caused a storm of angry protest. His work had a strength and directness that shocked many people. But today Epstein is recognized as one of the most important sculptors of his time. His sculptures are still exciting, even though they are no longer so shocking.

◄Jacob Epstein, British sculptor (left). An American Soldier *by Jacob Epstein* (right). *National Gallery of Art, Washington D.C., Gift of Rupert L. Joseph.*

Epstein was born in New York City of Russian-Polish parents. He became interested in art as a child and enjoyed making sketches of his neighborhood. As a young man he got a job in a bronze factory, where he learned to cast sculpture in bronze.

Epstein later studied art in Paris. One of his teachers was the great French sculptor, Auguste Rodin. Epstein also studied the collections at major art museums. He especially liked the primitive carved figures from Africa and ancient Egypt. His early sculptures were large, bulky figures carved in smooth stone. Parts of the bodies were exaggerated. His later work was modeled in clay and then cast in bronze. He would push and punch the clay to get a rough, rugged surface. This roughness makes the sculpture appear more alive.

Epstein settled in England in 1905 and became a British citizen. He was knighted by Queen Elizabeth II in 1954 for his contributions to art.

ALSO READ: RODIN, AUGUSTE; SCULPTURE.

EQUATOR The equator is an imaginary line around the middle of the Earth. Until recently, people thought that at every point the equator is an equal distance from the North and South poles. The equator is 24,830 miles long. A few years ago, space satellites made precise measurements of the Earth. The distance from the equator to the North Pole was found to be a little longer than from the equator to the South Pole. The equator, therefore, is not really at an equal distance from the North and South poles at every point. It is slightly closer to the South Pole. But the difference is so small that you can accept the definition given above.

The equator divides Earth into two halves, a Northern Hemisphere and a Southern Hemisphere. For most of its length, the equator runs across empty oceans. The lands it crosses are

▼A signboard marks the spot where the imaginary line of the equator passes through Kenya in eastern Africa.

northern South America, central Africa, and the Indonesian islands of Sumatra, Borneo, and Celebes (Sulawesi).

Most places near the equator have a hot climate, because the sun's rays fall directly upon the area. Some places at high altitudes on the equator have cooler climates, however. Manaus, Brazil, with an elevation of 105 feet above sea level, has an annual average temperature of 81 degrees. But Quito, Ecuador, located high in the Andes Mountains, has an annual temperature of 59 degrees. The sun's rays fall at an angle upon those areas located away from the equator. Most places away from the equator have lower annual average temperatures.

ALSO READ: CLIMATE, EARTH, GEOGRAPHY, LATITUDE AND LONGITUDE.

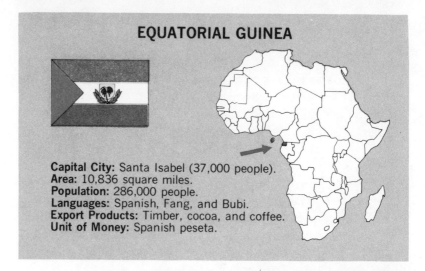

EQUATORIAL GUINEA

Capital City: Santa Isabel (37,000 people).
Area: 10,836 square miles.
Population: 286,000 people.
Languages: Spanish, Fang, and Bubi.
Export Products: Timber, cocoa, and coffee.
Unit of Money: Spanish peseta.

EQUATORIAL GUINEA The Republic of Equatorial Guinea has two parts. One is a small piece of land—about the size of the state of Maryland—on the west coast of Africa, between Cameroon and Gabon. This is called the Province of Rio Muni. The other part consists of two islands, Fernando Po and tiny Annobon, a few hundred miles off the African coast in the Gulf of Guinea. This part is called the Province of Fernando Po. (See the map with the article on AFRICA.)

The Province of Rio Muni, on the African mainland, is covered with jungles of huge ebony and mahogany trees. It has a narrow strip of white, sandy beaches. The climate is very hot and rainy. The capital city, Santa Isabel, on the island of Fernando Po, is the largest city. Some of the world's best cocoa comes from the cacao trees that grow in the island's fertile soil.

More than half of the Equatorial Guineans are Roman Catholics. Most of them own farms, although some make their living at lumbering. Many mainland children go to primary schools. School attendance is higher in Equatorial Guinea than in neighboring countries.

Fishing in the deep blue water surrounding the island of Fernando Po in Equatorial Guinea.

Equatorial Guinea was once called Spanish Guinea. The Island of Fernando Po is named after the Portuguese explorer who discovered it in the late 1400s. The country became a Spanish territory in 1778. It became independent, as Equatorial Guinea, on October 12, 1968. The republic is run by a president and a 35-member national assembly. Two councils run the business of its provinces. The citizens elect the president, the assembly, and the two councils.

ALSO READ: AFRICA.

EROSION Millions of years ago, mountains as high as the Rockies towered over what are today northern Minnesota, Wisconsin, and Michigan. Only low hills are left now. The ancient mountains were worn down by erosion, the action of running water, wind, and moving ice.

In erosion by water, flowing water rolls, scrapes, and bumps small pieces of rock along the bottom of a stream or river bed, and throws the rocks against the sides. This knocks other pieces of rock out of the bed, deepening and widening it. The current carries the smaller pieces downstream. This action goes on for millions of years, wearing down whole mountains and creating valleys and canyons, such as the mile-deep Grand Canyon.

A raindrop is like a tiny bomb striking the soil and splashing it upward. Rainwater flowing over the surface carries loosened soil away. The best way to prevent erosion of soil is by growing plants in it. Leaves break the fall of raindrops, and plant roots anchor the soil and absorb most of the water. People who chop down trees to clear a piece of land—and then do not plant anything in the soil—are speeding up the natural erosion process. Fertile soil is washed away in a short period of time, leaving behind deep gulleys and poor soil.

Wind erodes the land by picking up grains of sand and hurling them against rocks. The hammering of the sand grains wears away rock. In another kind of wind erosion, wind also blows away topsoil, if it is not anchored by the roots of plants.

Glaciers are sheets and rivers of moving ice. They erode the land by carrying along sand, pebbles, and large rocks. These

Badly eroded suburban land. Rain washed away the topsoil and created this barren gully. Good plant cover would have helped the soil to absorb the water.

The Dust Bowl is a region in the Great Plains where rain and wind eroded the rich soil because people used poor farming methods. During the 1930s, the soil vanished in terrible dust storms, causing many people to flee their farms.

collect at the bottom of the ice. The sand and rocks act like sandpaper, scraping away the surface of the earth over which the glacier moves. Over thousands of years glacial erosion wears down whole mountains, making deep, wide valleys.

To test the way ice can scratch and erode things, try this experiment. Ask your mother or teacher if you may use the ice box to make some special ice cubes. You will need three ice cube trays, two bowls, two big spoons, sawdust, and sand. Fill the first tray with water, the way ice cubes are made. In a bowl, make a mixture of a great deal of sawdust and a small amount of water. Stir the mixture until it looks somewhat like oatmeal and pour it into the ice cube tray. In another bowl, make a mixture containing a lot of sand and just enough water so that it looks like very thick soup. Pour the sand mixture into the third ice cube tray. Set the trays to freeze in the ice box.

When the cubes are frozen, perform the first test. Place one of each kind of ice cube in a saucer or a shallow pan. Which kind of cube melts first at room temperature?

Take one of each kind of cube outside. Which one is the easiest to break on the sidewalk?

Find the kind of plastic glass used at parties and often thrown out afterwards, like a paper cup. Which ice cubes scratch the plastic—the ordinary cube, or the special cubes? How does the sliding ice of a glacier work to cause erosion?

ALSO READ: CANYON, CONSERVATION, ECOLOGY, GLACIER, GRAND CANYON, ICE AGE, SOIL, WIND.

ESCALATOR see ELEVATORS AND ESCALATORS.

ESKIMO Eskimos have lived for centuries along the coasts of the Arctic Ocean, in Greenland, Canada, Alaska, and the Soviet Union. Their homeland is a vast region of approximately 3,200 miles, one of the most thinly populated regions on earth. Many people think the Eskimos originally lived in Siberia. They believe that the Eskimos migrated from this area across northern Canada to Greenland.

The name Eskimo means "eater of raw flesh." The Algonkin Indians originally gave the Eskimos their name. The Eskimos called themselves *Innuit*, meaning "men."

The Greenland Eskimos live in southern Greenland, and the Polar Eskimos live in northern Greenland. The Central Eskimos live in northern Canada. The Labrador, MacKenzie River, and Banks Island Eskimos live in other parts of Canada. Alaskan Eskimos live in Alaska, and Siberian Eskimos live in the northeastern part of the Soviet Union.

Eskimos are short. Few of them are more than 5 feet, 6 inches tall. They have heavy-set bodies. Their round faces have narrow eyes and high cheekbones. Eskimos' hair is jet black, and the color of their skin varies from light to dark brown.

The Eskimos have their own kind of "ice cream." They make it by mixing seal oil and sometimes reindeer tallow with snow and with berries that are in season.

◄ Eskimos fishing through holes in the ice. The three fishermen will load their catch on the sled and push it to their home.

Eskimos sometimes use rifles today, but they also use weapons they developed a long time ago—harpoons for hunting seals and walruses, for instance. For ice fishing, Eskimos cut a hole in the ice, sit by it, and spear fish swimming by. They also catch fish with hooks and nets.

Food supplies vary from one part of the Eskimos' homeland to another. Alaskan Eskimos have always eaten fish, as well as seal, whale, and berries. They now eat some canned foods and packaged cereals that come from the United States, as well as sugar, tea, and coffee. Eskimos living in northern Canada eat caribou, along with bear, some fish, birds, and plants. They also eat some canned and packaged foods from southern Canada. Walruses are killed for food. The Eskimos eat the dead animals' flesh, as well as the organs and fat. By eating so many parts of the animals, they get needed vitamins and minerals.

Parts of animals not eaten by man are used for other purposes. Seals have been used for dog food, clothing, needles, boats, tents, harpoons, and fuel for oil lamps. Caribou skins are used for clothing. Walrus tusks and skin are not allowed to go to waste. The tusks are often carved, and the skin is used for making boats called *kayaks*.

Eskimos call any form of shelter an *igloo*. The frozen snow houses we think of as igloos are used only by a few Canadian Eskimos. An igloo is made out of blocks of hard snow cut from the ground with knives. The Eskimos pile up the blocks to form a round house, big enough for one family to live in. These homes are quite warm inside, even though they are made from snow. Eskimos living in Greenland make houses from stone. Alaskan Eskimos build homes from lumber. They used to have

▼ An Eskimo props up his kayak to dry. A harpoon for catching seals and fish lies on the right side of the kayak.

▶ *A Canadian Eskimo igloo. Blocks of hard snow are fitted together in an upward spiral. The views here from above and from the side of an igloo show (1) the entrance, away from the wind, made to trap cold air; (2) the fur-covered sleeping shelf; and (3) the storage area below entrance level.*

houses made from turf that were partly underground. Summer dwellings are often tents, called *tupeks,* made from sealskin. Eskimo dress is the same for both men and women. They wear waterproof boots, called *mukluks,* trousers, and a jacket with a hood, called an *anorak* or *parka.* The hood can be drawn up to cover the head. The hood also forms a type of cradle for women to carry young babies on their backs.

In wintertime, most Eskimos travel and move supplies on sleds pulled by dogs. The sleds have runners made from ivory, whalebone, or iron.

The ice covering the Arctic Ocean melts in the summer. The Eskimos can then hunt seals and fish from canoe-like boats called *kayaks.* The frame of the kayak is made of seal bones or whale bones. The Eskimos sew sealskin all around the frame. They leave an opening on top so that a man can sit in the kayak. Whale hunters use a larger open boat called a *umiak.*

Eskimos are outstanding craftsmen. They carve walrus tusks to make pictures of birds and animals. They also carve designs on the tools they make. Some Eskimos make wooden masks— once used for religious ceremonies.

When the Eskimos came in contact with white men, their way of life began to change. Eskimos were not immune to the white men's diseases. Some of these diseases killed many Eskimos. The Eskimo language, which is understood by nearly all Eskimos, has changed. It includes some of the white men's words.

Many North American Eskimos live in towns today and have abandoned their old customs. They find jobs in mining, construction work, fish canning, and at defense bases in the far north. Their children go to modern schools, learning to read and write English.

ALSO READ: ALASKA; ARCTIC LIFE; CANADA; GREENLAND; INDIAN ART, AMERICAN; INDIANS, AMERICAN; NEWFOUNDLAND-LABRADOR; SOVIET UNION.

To see whales that were far out in the ocean, Eskimos held the edges of a sealskin and tossed a man as high as 40 feet into the air by bouncing him on the skin. He could then see much farther out to sea.

ESTEVANICO (1510–1539)   A black man was one of the earliest explorers of the southwest United States. His name means "Little Stephen" in Spanish. Estevanico came from Spain to America as a slave in 1528 with an expedition led by his owner, Panfilo de Narvaez. Only about 15 men had survived the expedition by the spring of 1529. Estevanico was one of them. They were captured by Indians in Texas and were held prisoner for five years. They pretended to be medicine men and "cured" some Indians by breathing on them and saying prayers. Estevanico and three others finally escaped. They traveled all the way to the Pacific coast of Mexico. In Mexico City, they amazed the Spanish with their tales of adventure. The Spanish sent Estevanico as a guide on an expedition to the north, led by a Franciscan monk named Friar Marcos de Niza. Estevanico discovered a Zuni Indian village called Cibola in what is now New Mexico. The Indians killed Estevanico, and Friar Marcos returned to Mexico City. The Spaniards thought Cibola was one of the "golden cities" they had heard of, but it was not. They sent a large expedition under Francisco Coronado to explore the area.

ALSO READ: CONQUISTADOR; CORONADO, FRANCISCO; EXPLORATION; NEGRO HISTORY.

ESTONIA   Estonia is one of fifteen republics in the Soviet Union. Its population of 1.2 million lives in an area smaller than Vermont and speaks a language similar to Finnish. It is located on the eastern coast of the Baltic Sea in northern Europe. Sweden and Finland are just across the Baltic Sea. Russia lies to the east, and Latvia forms the southern boundary. (See the map with the article on EUROPE.) Tallinn is the capital of Estonia. It was founded many years ago as a fortress.

Estonia has a moderate climate for a northern country. The sea water near its shores sometimes freezes in the winter, and

ESTONIA

Capital City: Tallinn (260,000 people).
Area: 17,400 square miles.
Population: 1,265,000 people.
Language: Estonian.
Export Products: Rye, wheat, and oats.
Unit of Money: Russian ruble.

▲ *Estonia's capital, Tallinn, is an ancient city of cobbled streets and medieval buildings. It is also a modern industrial center and the country's chief port.*

ships cannot reach the harbors. Special ships called icebreakers are used to cut channels through the ice. Estonia is famous for its many beautiful lakes. It also has many swampy marshlands. Much of Estonia is forest, with pine, spruce, birch, and fir trees. Lumber production is an important industry.

The soil of Estonia is very poor. Crops can grow only if the farmers use much fertilizer. The main crops are wheat and rye. Many farmers also raise pigs and cattle. Fishing, shipbuilding, mining, textiles, and machinery are important industries.

The Estonian people have always wanted to be independent, but they have not been strong enough to defend themselves against their neighbors. Other countries have usually ruled Estonia. In the past 1,000 years, the Estonians have been independent for only 22 years. The Danes and Germans conquered Estonia in the Middle Ages. Sweden took over the area in the sixteenth century. Russia drove out the Swedes in 1721. Estonia became independent of Russia in 1918, but Russia took over again in 1940. The Germans invaded the country the following year and held it until 1944. The Estonians are now officially Soviet (Russian) citizens, but they still consider themselves Estonians. Some countries, including the United States, do not recognize the Soviet take-over of Estonia.

ALSO READ: SOVIET UNION.

ESTUARY see RIVER, SEACOAST.

▼ The Knight, Death, and the Devil, *an engraving by Albrecht Durer. National Gallery of Arts Washington, D.C., Gift of W. G. Russell Allen.*

ETCHING AND ENGRAVING   Etching and engraving are ways of making a picture on a flat piece of glass or metal, called a *plate*. The plate is most often made of copper. The plate is then used to make a *print* on paper. Several prints can be made from a plate before it is destroyed. Many famous collections of prints belong to art museums in North America and Europe. They are not displayed so often as paintings, however. They fade easily, and must be exhibited in proper lighting.

Making an Engraving

To make an engraving, an artist takes a pointed tool called a *burin*, and cuts his design into the plate. He rubs ink over the plate, then wipes off all of it except the part that sinks into the lines made by the burin. He presses the plate very hard against a piece of paper. The ink that has stayed in the lines is squeezed on to the paper to make the print. An artist must learn to handle the burin delicately and control the depth of the lines.

One of the greatest engravers of all time was the German artist, Albrecht Durer (1471–1528). He was born in Nuremberg, the son of a goldsmith. Most artists at that time were putting beautiful, idealized people in their paintings and drawings. But Durer drew people as he really saw them, and sometimes exaggerated ugly or unusual features. His engravings—often of imaginary scenes—are powerful and convincing. One of his most famous engravings is on the previous page—*The Knight, Death, and the Devil*. Durer made this engraving as a plea to the Dutch philosopher Erasmus, urging him to begin reforms in the Roman Catholic church, which had become very corrupt.

Making an Etching

Etching is a technique similar to engraving. The artist covers a plate with wax, then draws on it with a needle. Wherever he moves his needle, the wax comes off and the surface of the plate is laid bare. He then puts the plate into an acid. The acid bites into the plate, so the drawing is transferred to the plate. The picture is then printed like an engraving. The technique of etching allows the artist to include more detail in his print.

The Dutch artist Rembrandt van Rijn made many beautiful etchings. He lived during the 1600s. A detail of one of his prints, *Christ Preaching*, is shown here. The lines of the print vividly portray the powerful personality of Christ.

◀ A detail of Christ Preaching, *an etching by Rembrandt van Rijn. National Gallery of Art, Washington, D.C., Gift of W. G. Russell Allen.*

▼ An aquatint etching by Francisco Goya.

The Spanish artist Francisco Goya did the other etching shown here. See how his etching differs from Rembrandt's. The slightly different technique is called *aquatint*. With this method, the artist could make not only etched lines but shaded patches as well. Many of Goya's etchings show his strong feelings about cruelty, lack of freedom, and stupidity. Here he makes fun of a young man in love—bowing and doffing his hat to a young lady who seems little interested. Two old ladies in the background gossip about the lovers.

Artists today still work in etching and engraving. New methods have been developed, but some artists still like to work on old-fashioned copper plates.

ALSO READ: ART HISTORY, GRAPHIC ARTS, REMBRANDT VAN RIJN.

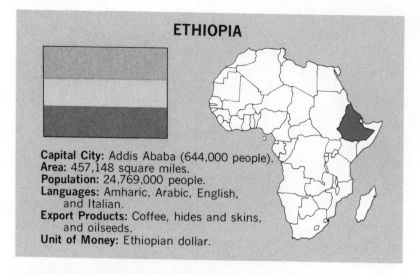

ETHIOPIA

Capital City: Addis Ababa (644,000 people).
Area: 457,148 square miles.
Population: 24,769,000 people.
Languages: Amharic, Arabic, English, and Italian.
Export Products: Coffee, hides and skins, and oilseeds.
Unit of Money: Ethiopian dollar.

ETHIOPIA　Ethiopia is a constitutional monarchy in northeastern Africa. It is one of the continent's larger nations—somewhat bigger than Texas, Oklahoma, and New Mexico combined. Ethiopia is a mountainous nation bordered by Sudan to the northwest, Kenya to the south, and Somalia to the south and east. The Red Sea forms the nation's northern boundary. The highest mountain, Ras Dashan, is 15,160 feet high and located in the northern part of the country. The Blue Nile, or Abbai, begins in Lake Tena. (See the map with the article on AFRICA.)

The climate is mild in much of the country where the altitude is high. The Red Sea coast is hot. The inland valleys and swamps are hot and humid.

The Ethiopians come from many different tribes. Today most Ethiopians live in rural areas. They raise a variety of products, among them coffee, grain, cotton, sugar cane, and oil seeds. They export mostly coffee, hides, grain, and oil seeds. Industry and mining are less important than agriculture. The majority of the people are illiterate (cannot read or write), even though many schools and a new university have been built.

▶ *The market place of the town of Harar, the capital of Harar Province in southeastern Ethiopia. Food, spices, and animals are sold in the market.*

The Ethiopian history is a long one. Some historians believe the Queen of Sheba, who visited Solomon (king of the ancient Hebrews), was Queen Maxeda of Axum. To this day, the ruler of Ethiopia has "the Lion of Judah" as part of his title. Historians know that the kingdom of Axum was still thriving in 500 B.C. Christian missionaries came to the country in the fourth century A.D., and about one-half of the population are Christians today. Native Ethiopians of the Christian faith are called *Copts* and belong to the Coptic Church.

Italy invaded Ethiopia in the 1890s and took over a piece of land, called Eritrea, as a colony. Italy invaded again in 1935 without declaring war. This time all of Ethiopia became an Italian colony. British troops and the Ethiopians freed the country in 1941 during World War II.

Emperor Haile Selassie was crowned in 1930 and continued to rule his country into the 1970s. He helped establish the Organization of African Unity in 1963. Its headquarters are in Addis Ababa, Ethiopia's capital.

ALSO READ: AFRICA.

ETRUSCAN Before the Romans came to power in Italy, an ancient people called the Etruscans lived there. They lived in the country of Etruria, the region of Italy now called Tuscany. The Greek word for Etruria was Tyrrhenia. Today the part of the Mediterranean Sea that lies southwest of Italy is called the Tyrrhenian Sea. Most historians think that the Etruscans came to Italy from Asia Minor around 1000 B.C. We know very little about these people. About 6,000 short sentences and names in the Etruscan language have been found on walls, statues, and vases. But so far, no one has been able to translate them.

The Etruscans built magnificent palaces and temples. Their underground tombs have beautiful paintings on plaster. They were skilled in making a black pottery known as *bucchero*. They created large and impressive statues of bronze, stone, and *terra cotta* (baked clay). Etruscan jewelry was especially lovely. Etruscans believed in many gods. They thought they could foresee the future by studying the insides of dead animals and by watching the flights of birds overhead.

Most Etruscans were traders and farmers. They became very rich and powerful and extended their lands from a small country to a large one. At the height of its power, about 535 B.C., Etruria covered most of northern Italy. It ruled Rome and greatly influenced the Roman way of life. With a strong army and navy, the Etruscans tried to conquer more land, but they were pushed back by the Gauls. In 396 B.C., the Etruscans lost a battle to Roman forces. Other battles followed, and by the 200s B.C., the Etruscans were completely under Roman rule.

ALSO READ: ANCIENT CIVILIZATIONS, ITALIAN HISTORY.

▲ *An Etruscan sculpture made of terra cotta, a ceramic clay. Etruscan sculptors preferred soft materials to express the happiness and gentleness of their figures, rather than the hard stone used by Greek sculptors.*

▲ *Many European buildings are centuries old. These hardy citizens of Zagorsk in Russia are passing by a building constructed in the Byzantine style more than 500 years ago.*

EUROPE   Europe is the second smallest of the continents, after Australia. Some geographers do not classify Europe as a continent at all. They consider it the western tip of Eurasia. (The name "Eurasia" combines the two names, Europe and Asia). But the landscapes, history, and cultural traditions of Europe are quite distinct from those of most of Asia.

Europe is separated from Asia by the low-lying Ural Mountains. It is bordered by water on the other three sides. Its northern coast is washed by the icy Arctic Ocean. The Atlantic Ocean lies to the west. Arms of the Atlantic cut into the land, forming bays and seas. The Mediterranean Sea is an arm of the Atlantic. It is part of Europe's southern boundary. The Baltic Sea and the North Sea, also arms of the Atlantic, flank the Scandinavian peninsula in the north. The oceans and seas around the continent have many islands, which are all considered part of Europe. Some are large and fertile, like Great Britain. Others are small and rocky, such as those along the Norwegian coast. Some, like Iceland, are far away from the continent.

Despite its small size, Europe has played a major part in the history of the world. Modern Western civilization began in Greece. Europeans were among the first people to travel and explore the world. They took their ideas about government, science, and religion with them. Thus, these ideas influenced people in places all over the world where Europeans settled.

The Land

Europe has four main geographical regions—the northwestern uplands, the Great European Plain, the central uplands, and the southern mountains.

▼ *A small fishing village in Norway. Seafood is an important part of the European diet. Russia, Norway, Spain, Iceland, and Britain are among the top twelve fishing nations of the world.*

The *northwestern uplands* are rugged, rocky hills that run through northwestern France, the British Isles, and Scandinavia. The coastlines of Norway and the British Isles are broken by beautiful narrow bays and inlets. These inlets are called *fiords* in Norway, and *firths* in the northern British Isles (Scotland). Iron and lead are among the minerals found in the rocky hills. In Scandinavia, the uplands are covered with forests of pine and spruce.

The *Great European Plain* lies south of the uplands. It starts as a narrow belt in the southeastern British Isles and sweeps eastward through northern France, Belgium, the Netherlands, northern Germany, part of Sweden, and Poland. The plain broadens to include Finland and the Soviet Union east of the Ural Mountains. Europe's longest river, the Volga, flows south across this region. It empties into the great saltwater lake known as the Caspian Sea. The Great European Plain is the most densely populated and the most fertile part of the continent. It has rich farmlands and forests of beech, ash, oak, and elm. Many of Europe's industrial cities are in this region.

The *central uplands* are a belt of high, flat hills that include part of France, Portugal, and Spain, and stretch through central Europe to Czechoslovakia. These uplands are less rugged than those in the northwest. Rivers have cut deep valleys into the hills. The region has poor soil, but dense forests of oak, beech, and ash grow in some areas. Europe's largest deposits of coal are in the central uplands. Two major rivers of France, the Seine and the Loire, rise in the French uplands.

The *southern mountains* are majestic, snow-covered ranges. Deep, flat valleys separate the mountain ranges. The valleys are dotted with towns and villages. To the east, a range called the Alps crosses Austria, Switzerland, northern Italy, and southeastern France. The Alps include some of the highest mountains in Europe. Two of the greatest rivers of Europe, the Rhine and the Danube, rise in the Alps. Further west, a range called the Pyrenees forms a natural boundary between France and Spain. Evergreen trees grow in the southern mountains. The whole mountain chain is also known as the Alpine System.

▲*Cattle are bred both for their meat and milk in most parts of Europe. Shown above is a high pasture in the Swiss Alps.*

The Climate

The climate of Europe varies from the cold, ice-bound northeastern regions to the hot, sunny Mediterranean. Many areas in between have a temperate climate—warm in the summer and cool in the winter. Most of these regions have enough rainfall to maintain rich farmlands and thick forests.

Animal Life

Many years ago, wild animals of many kinds roamed the forests and plains of Europe. As time went by, hunters killed off many of them. The remaining animals had fewer places to live as

Europe is named after Europa, a Phoenician princess in Greek mythology. Europa climbed on the back of a white bull, who leaped into the sea and carried her to the island Crete. The bull was really the god Zeus in disguise.

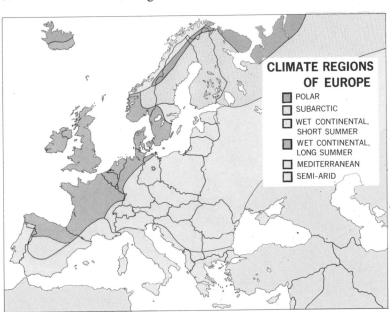

CLIMATE REGIONS OF EUROPE

- POLAR
- SUBARCTIC
- WET CONTINENTAL, SHORT SUMMER
- WET CONTINENTAL, LONG SUMMER
- MEDITERRANEAN
- SEMI-ARID

EUROPEAN NATIONS

COUNTRY	AREA IN SQUARE MILES	CAPITAL	COUNTRY'S POPULATION
ALBANIA	11,096	Tirane	2,075,000
ANDORRA	175	Andorra la Vella	19,000
AUSTRIA	32,369	Vienna	7,371,000
BELGIUM	11,775	Brussels	9,646,000
BULGARIA	42,796	Sofia	8,436,000
CZECHOSLOVAKIA	49,356	Prague	14,418,000
DENMARK	16,556	Copenhagen	4,910,000
ESTONIA	17,400	Tallinn	1,265,000
FINLAND	130,500	Helsinki	4,703,000
FRANCE	212,736	Paris	50,320,000
GERMANY (EAST)	41,535	East Berlin	16,010,000
GERMANY (WEST)	95,914	Bonn	58,707,000
GIBRALTAR	2	Gibraltar	27,000
GREAT BRITAIN	94,214	London	55,534,000
GREECE	51,182	Athens	8,835,000
HUNGARY	35,875	Budapest	10,295,000
ICELAND	39,709	Reykjavik	203,000
IRELAND (SOUTH)	26,601	Dublin	2,921,000
ITALY	116,286	Rome	53,170,000
LATVIA	24,600	Riga	2,229,000
LIECHTENSTEIN	65	Vaduz	21,000
LITHUANIA	25,200	Vilna	2,926,000
LUXEMBOURG	999	Luxembourg	337,000
MALTA	122	Valletta	323,000
MONACO	.58	Monaco	23,000
NETHERLANDS	12,883	Amsterdam	12,873,000
NORWAY	124,560	Oslo	3,851,000
POLAND	119,734	Warsaw	32,555,000
PORTUGAL	35,413	Lisbon	9,560,000
RUMANIA	91,671	Bucharest	20,010,000
SAN MARINO	38	San Marino	19,000
SOVIET UNION*	8,570,600	Moscow	240,571,000
SPAIN	195,258	Madrid	32,949,000
SWEDEN	173,394	Stockholm	7,978,000
SWITZERLAND	15,944	Bern	6,230,000
YUGOSLAVIA	99,079	Belgrade	20,351,000

*The bulk of the Soviet Union (U.S.S.R.) is in Asia but its capital is in Europe, so that nation is listed with European countries.

▲*An old man relaxes with his pet pelican on the island of Mykonos, a European beauty spot which lies off the southern coast of Greece.*

▼*Open air food markets are commonplace in many European cities. The food, locally grown, is often fresher and cheaper than supermarket produce. This street market is in London, England.*

more land was cleared for farms and towns. Bison and wild boar have almost disappeared. Wolves, brown bears, lynxes, and wolverines are still seen in some parts of Europe. But the most common animals today are foxes, rabbits, hares, squirrels, and deer.

The number of different birds living in Europe is also growing smaller. The continent was once rich in eagles, wild ducks, storks, and geese. But now, skylarks, finches, nightingales, doves, and sparrows are among the most common birds. The seas around Europe have numerous kinds of fish. Rivers and lakes in many parts of Europe are famous for their trout and salmon.

The People

Man probably first came to Europe from Asia and Africa many thousands of years ago. Today, people throughout large areas of the continent share similar physical characteristics. Many people of northern Europe have fair skin, blonde hair, and blue eyes. People of central Europe and the Alps often have brown hair, brown eyes, and stocky bodies. Many people living in countries along the Mediterranean coast have dark hair, dark eyes, and a small build. Europe is now divided into many countries, each with its own national characteristics. No common language is spoken in Europe. But English, French, and German are understood in most countries.

Europe is one of the most densely populated areas of the world. For many years, the land could not produce all the food the people needed. Today, modern farming methods make it possible to grow more food. In addition, ships bring food to Europe from other parts of the world.

As other regions of the world were explored, many families left Europe to make a living elsewhere. Other people left in search of political or religious freedom. Millions of Europeans came to North America. Many others went to South America, Australia, and Africa.

Europeans at Work

Europe is highly industrialized. Industrial development has been possible because the continent is rich in raw materials. A vast network of transportation routes has also been built up over hundreds of years. European factories were the first to use machine power instead of human labor in the great series of changes called the *Industrial Revolution*. The most heavily industrialized areas are now in the Soviet Union, East and West Germany, Great Britain, France, and Italy.

New agricultural machinery was also invented during the Industrial Revolution. Farmers found that they could grow more and better crops by using fertilizers. Belgium, the Nether-

◀ Automobile manufacturing is an important industry in France, Britain, Sweden, West Germany, and Italy. Many of these Fiat cars coming off an assembly line in Italy will be sold in North America.

lands, Denmark, and France became important farming areas. Major agricultural products include wheat, vegetables, fruit, and dairy produce.

The land along the mountainous coast of the Mediterranean is too poor to grow cereal crops. But oranges, lemons, grapes, and olives ripen well on the sunny hillsides. Famous wines are produced from the grapes grown in this region and in other parts of France, Italy, and western Germany. The heavily forested lands of northern Europe are equally poor for crops, but these regions are famous for their timber.

History

The first great European civilization began in ancient Greece. The people of the Greek city of Athens originated the idea of democratic government. Greek artists, philosophers, and scientists left a rich heritage of knowledge and art.

Rome began to grow in power and wealth a few centuries before the birth of Jesus Christ. All of western Europe and the lands around the Mediterranean became part of the Roman

◀ The old ways of life still persist in parts of Europe. In some rural areas of Spain the horse and cart, not the automobile, are used for transportation.

▲The ruins of an ancient Greek theater in Syracuse, Sicily. Signs of ancient times remain all over Europe.

Empire. Romans wrote strict laws for the government of this huge empire. Many modern countries base their laws on those of ancient Rome. The Roman language, Latin, is the basis of many European languages today.

Belief in Christianity spread slowly through Europe following the death of Christ around 29 A.D. The early Christians were persecuted, but the new religion attracted many converts. Christianity had become the official religion of the Roman Empire by 400 A.D. It is still the most widespread religion in Europe.

Fierce Germanic tribes from central and northern Europe attacked the Roman Empire during the 300s and 400s A.D. The Roman Empire began to collapse. The period of time between the destruction of the Roman Empire and the late 1400s is often called the Middle Ages. Kings and noblemen fought to gain control of the lands that were once part of the Roman Empire. Society was organized in a system known as *feudalism.* Under the feudal system, the nobles often became extremely powerful. But one king, Charlemagne, built up a large kingdom in present-day France, Italy, and Germany. He was the first ruler to bring peace and order to Europe since the fall of the empire.

During the Middle Ages, the Roman Catholic Church was the only steady and dependable authority in Europe. The power of the Church increased, and many people were converted to Christianity. Several European kings and nobles led expeditions to the Middle East to fight for control of the Holy Land. These expeditions, known as the *Crusades,* lasted from the 1000s to the 1200s.

By the 1300s, the feudal system was breaking up. Individual rulers were gaining control over large areas of land. The countries of Europe, as we know them today, were beginning to be formed. Trade between Europe and the Middle East had increased as a result of the Crusades. European cities grew larger, and merchants became interested in finding new trade routes. The Spaniards and Portuguese were among the first to explore the coast of Africa, reach Asia, and sail to the New World.

The period known as the *Renaissance* began in Italy before 1500. It was a time in which many new ideas in art, architecture, science, philosophy, literature, and politics developed. Members of the Roman Catholic Church began to disagree on various aspects of Christianity. One group of people split away from the Church during a period known as the Reformation. They formed the Protestant Church. For many years, Protestants and Catholics fought religious wars against one another.

Many wars have been fought in Europe. These have usually been between different countries, but sometimes, people within a country disagreed with their king or ruler and began a revolution. One of the most important revolutions took place in France between 1789 and 1799. The French king was beheaded, and France became a republic. Several other European countries have since become republics. Some have managed to do this peacefully.

France, Germany, Austria, Great Britain, and Russia became great powers during the 1800s and early 1900s. Their jealous rivalry led to the outbreak of World War I. This war lasted from 1914 to 1918, when Germany and her allies were defeated. During this period, a revolution broke out in Russia. The Russians overthrew their czar (emperor) and established a Communist government, the Soviet Union, in 1917. Peace did not last long in Europe after World War I. Germany and her allies fought other European nations again in World War II, between 1939 and 1945.

Europe has been divided into two factions, or *blocs,* since 1945. The Soviet Union and the nations of Eastern Europe are Communist countries. Most of the nations in Western Europe are democratic countries. The hostility between the two groups is often called the "Cold War." Many of the nations of Western Europe are united in a defensive system called the North Atlantic Treaty Organization (NATO). A trading association called the European Economic Community (EEC), or the Common Market, has also been formed among several Western European countries.

For further information on:

Cities, *see* AMSTERDAM, ATHENS, BERLIN, FLORENCE, LONDON, MOSCOW, PARIS, ROME, VENICE.

History, *see* ART HISTORY; CRUSADES; ENGLISH HISTORY; FEUDALISM; FRENCH HISTORY; FRENCH REVOLUTION; GERMAN HISTORY; GREECE, ANCIENT; HOLY ROMAN EMPIRE; INDUSTRIAL REVOLUTION; ITALIAN HISTORY; KINGS AND QUEENS; MIDDLE AGES; PROTESTANT REFORMATION; RENAISSANCE; REPUBLIC; REVOLUTION; ROMAN EMPIRE; RUSSIAN HISTORY; SPANISH HISTORY; WAR OF 1812; WORLD WAR I; WORLD WAR II.

Languages, *see* ENGLISH LANGUAGE, GERMAN LANGUAGE, GREEK, LANGUAGES, LATIN, ROMANCE LANGUAGES, RUSSIAN LANGUAGE, SCANDINAVIAN LANGUAGES.

Organizations, *see* COMMON MARKET, NORTH ATLANTIC TREATY ORGANIZATION.

Physical Features, *see* ADRIATIC SEA, AEGEAN SEA, ALPS MOUNTAINS, BALTIC SEA, BLACK SEA, CASPIAN SEA, CAUCASUS MOUNTAINS, DANUBE RIVER, ENGLISH CHANNEL, MEDITERRANEAN SEA, NORTH SEA, RHINE RIVER, THAMES RIVER, URAL MOUNTAINS.

Travel, *see* BIG BEN, LEANING TOWER OF PISA, LOUVRE, STONEHENGE, TOWER OF LONDON, VERSAILLES, WESTMINSTER ABBEY.

Also read the article on each country listed in the table.

EUROPE

Highest Point: Mount Elbrus in Soviet Union—18,481 feet.

Lowest Point: Caspian Sea, located mainly in southwest Soviet Union—92 feet below sea level.

Longest River: Volga River —2,300 miles long.

Biggest Lake: Lake Ladoga in Soviet Union— 7,100 miles long.

Largest City: Paris (8,197,000 people).

Total Population: 703,000,000 people.

EVANGELIST

▲ *The Reverend Billy Graham is one of the most popular evangelists. He speaks to large crowds of people and reaches many more people through radio and television broadcasts.*

EVANGELIST A person who travels from place to place, preaching the gospel, or the teachings of Jesus Christ, is called an evangelist. Evangelists are also called *revivalists.* The meetings at which they preach are called *revival meetings.* Evangelists hope to bring about a revival (or renewal) of religious faith.

Four of Christ's disciples, Matthew, Mark, Luke, and John, were the first evangelists. After the death of Christ, they traveled around, preaching his message and telling about his life. They were called "evangelists." The Greek word *evangelion* means "good news," and these disciples were preaching the "good news about Christ." Their written accounts of the life and teachings of Christ became the first four books of the New Testament. The word for "good news" in Old English was *gospel,* the message preached by the four evangelists.

Most modern evangelists are Protestants. Evangelists may be either men or women. Some evangelists are *ordained ministers.* An ordained minister has received intensive training not only in the principles and practices of his religion, but often in related fields, such as philosophy and psychology. There is usually an ordination ceremony. Evangelists who are not ordained are called *lay preachers.*

The Methodist Church was founded by the famous British evangelist John Wesley. Billy Graham is the best-known American evangelist today. He has preached to millions of people throughout the world. Many of his revival meetings are shown on television.

ALSO READ: BIBLE; MISSIONARY; PROTESTANT CHURCHES; RELIGION; WESLEY, JOHN AND CHARLES.

EVERGLADES Southern Florida boasts the largest, shallowest, and most unusual marshland in America—the Everglades. This flat, swampy region covers more than 5,000 square miles. It stretches about 100 miles, from Lake Okeechobee to the tip of the Florida peninsula. Its swamps are usually no deeper than nine inches.

The soil of the Everglades is largely peat. This is dark, rich soil formed by decayed plant matter. It makes excellent farmland when drained. The Florida government began work on draining the area in 1906. The Federal Government has also helped Florida to build canals and dikes for drainage and flood control. This work has made it possible to grow sugar cane and vegetables along the shores of Lake Okeechobee.

The best way to travel in the Everglades is in an airboat. An airboat is a flat-bottomed boat with an air propeller and a rudder like an airplane. Imagine that you are on an airboat piloted by a Florida ranger. As the boat gains speed, sawgrass slaps the metal sides of the boat, then folds down in front as the boat rides along on a cushion of grass and water. Sawgrass is a sharp-edged grass that can grow as high as 12 feet. The ranger sits in a high seat to see above the sawgrass. Here and there amid this "sea" of grass are islands of soil, covered with tropical plants and trees, such as palms and gumbo-limbo trees.

In the Everglades, you can see wildlife all around. An alligator may be half buried in a mudhole, sheltered from the hot sun. Long-legged herons and white-plumed egrets look for fish to eat. Raccoons and otters play. The small, hawk-like Everglades kite feeds on snails, spearing them with its hooked beak.

The rangers spend part of their time searching for people who kill alligators. Alligators are hunted for their skins. In recent years, some 50,000 alligators were illegally killed in Florida. Stiff new laws are helping to stop this slaughter.

ALSO READ: FLORIDA, NATIONAL PARK.

◄A peaceful scene on the Tamiami Trail in the Everglades National Park which covers the southwestern tip of the Florida Everglades. The area is rich in animal and plant life.

EVERGREEN TREE   If you live in a region where the winters are very cold, you know that many trees shed their leaves in the fall. Their branches are bare by the time winter comes. Trees that lose their leaves for the winter are called *deciduous* trees. Other trees have leaves all winter long, no matter how cold it gets. These are called evergreen trees. Pines, spruces, hemlocks, and firs are among the most familiar evergreens. They are all members of a family of cone-bearing trees called *conifers.* Small pines and firs are popular as Christmas trees. The leaves of evergreen conifers are called *needles,* because of their long, narrow shape. The shape of the needles makes them able to stand the low temperatures and harsh winds of winter. Evergreens do shed their needles at times. But they usually shed them a few at a time, throughout the year, not all at once. New needles grow to take the place of those that drop off. If you walk through an evergreen forest, you will see many brown, dried-up needles scattered about the ground.

▲ *A holly bush is an ever-green that is a popular decoration at Christmas.*

Other kinds of evergreens have broad leaves instead of needle-shaped leaves. These evergreens usually live in places where winters are not very cold. Some types of live oak and the magnolia that grow in southern parts of the United States are broad-leafed evergreens. Other kinds of oak and magnolia are deciduous. The American holly is found from Maine to Florida and as far west as southern Texas. The holly's shiny, dark green leaves and bright red berries are used to make attractive wreaths at Christmastime.

ALSO READ: CONIFER, PLANT, PLANT DISTRIBUTION, TREE.

EVOLUTION   You probably have seen pictures of the huge lizards called *dinosaurs,* or perhaps you have seen dinosaur skeletons in a museum. No dinosaurs are alive today. Thousands of other kinds of animals and plants lived for a time and then disappeared. What happened to them?

There has been a long chain of life from the first one-celled living things to the plants and animals of today. Why did some kinds of living things die out, and others survive? How did living things change from single cells to the complicated plants and animals of today? The answers to these questions make up the study of *evolution*.

Evolution is Change

▼ *The struggle for existence meant that those animals that were best equipped survived. Giraffes probably developed from ancestors that were accidentally born with longer necks and could take advantage of food that other animals could not reach.*

Evolution tries to explain the origin and development of the many kinds of animals and plants that are on Earth today and were on Earth in previous times. (Animals and plants that do not exist anymore are known because of their fossil remains.) The theory of evolution includes two main ideas. (1) Living things change from generation to generation. Over a long period of time, the offspring begin to take on new characteristics. This process has been going on for a very long time, and it has produced all the groups of plants and animals that have ever lived. (2) All living things are probably related, through ancestors they have in common. For example, evolutionists think that men and apes probably descended, through millions of years, from the same kind of animal.

Man has wondered why so many different kinds of plants and animals exist. Many people have searched for answers. Since ancient times, thinkers have noticed that plants and animals change. None of them was able to suggest any reasons that agreed with the way nature works. Almost 175 years ago, a great French naturalist, Jean de Lamarck, put forth a theory of change in living things. His theory was made up of several ideas:

(1) Part of a plant or animal can be changed by use or disuse. For example, a giraffe reaching for leaves high on a tree could permanently stretch its neck a little. The slightly longer neck

could then be passed on to the giraffe's offspring. This is a change caused by use. On the other hand, whales came from ancestors that lived on land and had four legs. When whales took to living in the sea, they had no use for legs. Their legs, through disuse, shriveled away.

(2) Animals and plants develop new parts that help them survive. If a giraffe needed leaves that are on higher branches for food, then it had to increase the length of its neck in order to survive.

(3) Characteristics acquired through use or disuse during the life of a plant or animal can be passed on to the offspring. Through many generations of use or disuse, changes resulted in new kinds of plants or animals.

Today we know that Lamarck's theory was not correct. Although use or disuse may cause a change, the change is very slight. And no matter how great the need, the change of a part is not assured. Many plants and animals that died might have lived, if they had been able to meet changes in their environment. For example, when the climate became cool all over the world, about 65 million years ago, many kinds of reptiles could not survive because they were unable to grow fur. Lastly, we know that characteristics acquired during an animal's lifetime are not passed on to its offspring. If the tails were cut off 50 generations of mice, the tails of the fifty-first generation would be no shorter than those of the first generation.

▲*The giant turtles found on the Galapagos Islands helped Charles Darwin form his theory of the origin of species. He found that the turtles on each island evolved some different characteristics which equipped them to survive in different environments.*

Darwin and Wallace

The first reasonable theory of evolution was put forth by Charles Darwin and Alfred Russel Wallace in 1858. Darwin, after years of study, was convinced that all living things came from common origins, but had changed a great deal through millions of years. Darwin presented his ideas, along with a great amount of supporting evidence, in a book titled *On the Origin of Species by Means of Natural Selection.* His ideas caused other scientists to re-examine their own ideas. Darwin gave several explanations for the process of evolution.

VARIATION. No two plants or animals are exactly alike. Among a litter of puppies, for example, one may have longer ears than the rest. Another may be brown, while the rest are black. Each generation has offspring that vary a little from their parents and from each other.

INHERITED VARIATIONS. Some variations that an individual is born with can be passed on to the offspring, and some cannot.

STRUGGLE FOR EXISTENCE. The offspring of any kind of plant or animal must struggle with others for food, water, sunlight, safety, and other necessary things. Many individual offspring fail in the struggle and die. A plant or animal must survive many dangers to live long enough to have offspring.

▲The Great Irish deer died out long ago because its ponderous antlers grew too big to be an advantage any longer. Only the fittest deer, who could make quick escapes from their enemies, survived. (Picture by Charles R. Knight, © Chicago Museum of Natural History.)

SURVIVAL OF THE FITTEST. The ways in which some individuals vary may give them an advantage in the struggle for existence. The advantage may be in getting food or escaping enemies. Plants and animals having these advantages will survive; others may not. If the surviving individuals can pass their advantage on to their offspring, the offspring will survive, too. These individuals are the fittest.

As a general rule, unfavorable variations are not passed on for many generations. Individuals having variations that fit them poorly for survival usually do not live long enough to have offspring. All the poorly fitted individuals soon die out. As a result of the struggle for existence, nature weeds out the unfit and preserves the fit.

NATURAL SELECTION OF NEW SPECIES. Small changes in fitness may add up to large changes over many generations. Eventually, the changes make an individual different enough to be called a new *species,* or kind. The individuals of the new species must be fitted for the struggle for existence, or they would not have survived. Since the individuals of the new, well-fitted species are different from their ancestors, the environment must have changed. The environment influenced, or selected, the new species. The process is called *natural selection.*

Let us see how the process of evolution worked with the camel. Millions of years ago, the earliest ancestor of the camel appeared in North America. It was about the size of a jackrabbit. When it ran, it leaped, because its front legs were so much shorter than its hind legs. This animal eventually developed into a llama-like creature about the size of a sheep. During the Miocene period, its descendant looked like the modern gazelle. This creature developed into the giraffe-sized camel of the middle Miocene (about 25 million years ago) and early Pliocene (about 13 million years ago) periods. By this time, the camel had developed a padded hoof for walking on sand. During the Pliocene period, these early camels migrated to Asia. There they developed, over many generations, other characteristics that helped them survive in hot, dry, sandy areas. The camel's teeth and stomach adapted to the dry grass and twigs available as food. It developed humps on its back to store large quantities of fat. In the desert, food and water are not always available. The camel's body can break this fat down into the food it needs. The camel's body tissues and pouches in its stomach help it retain water. The camel also developed several characteristics to protect itself from sand. It has two rows of eyelashes and hairy ear openings. And it can close its nostrils.

Other Scientists Study Evolution

Darwin did not understand why or how variations in plants and animals occurred. No one else seemed to know. But just about the time that Darwin was presenting his theory of natural selection, an Austrian monk, Gregor Mendel, was finding the answer to how variations occur. Mendel was carrying out breeding experiments with peas. He kept a careful record of the characteristics of parents and offspring of several generations. He was able to work out how many individuals in a generation would vary, and what variations might be expected. He showed that inheritance takes place in an orderly manner, and that both parents contribute equally to the characteristics their offspring inherit. Mendel published his work in 1866, but unfortunately, no one paid attention to it for more than 35 years.

A German biologist, August Weismann, showed that these inherited variations resulted from changes in sex cells (sperm or

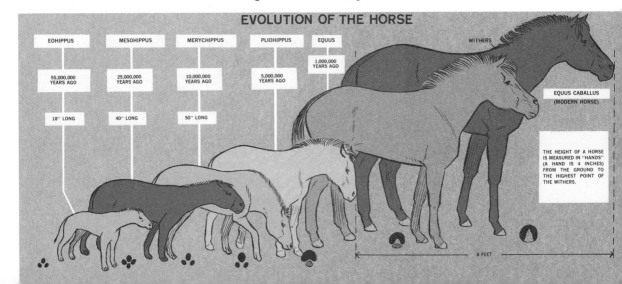

EVOLUTION OF THE HORSE

| EOHIPPUS | MESOHIPPUS | MERYCHIPPUS | PLIOHIPPUS | EQUUS | | WITHERS |

1,000,000 YEARS AGO

55,000,000 YEARS AGO   25,000,000 YEARS AGO   10,000,000 YEARS AGO   5,000,000 YEARS AGO

EQUUS CABALLUS (MODERN HORSE)

18" LONG   40" LONG   50" LONG

THE HEIGHT OF A HORSE IS MEASURED IN "HANDS" (A HAND IS 4 INCHES) FROM THE GROUND TO THE HIGHEST POINT OF THE WITHERS.

8 FEET

egg), not in any of the other cells in a plant or animal.

A Dutch botanist, Hugo de Vries, found in 1901 that small changes can occur suddenly, in a single generation. He called these changes *mutations.* He found that some mutations were passed on to the next generation. He concluded that these mutations were the reason for new variations in evolution.

Natural selection then determines whether a mutation benefits an individual in the struggle for existence. And this, in turn, decides whether a mutation that can be inherited will be passed on to many future generations.

Scientists found that in each living cell there are tangled threads of matter. These are *chromosomes.* Each chromosome is made up of a number of small units called *genes.* It is the genes that determine what characteristics individuals will inherit. Each gene is a giant molecule. The arrangement of atoms in the gene molecule can be changed by high-energy radiation (such as X-rays), heat, and chemicals. When these atoms are rearranged, a *mutation* probably will result in the next generation.

No one theory gives all the answers to the question of evolution. One of the most important facts about evolution is that all the facts are not known. If you decide to work in this area of science, you might find the fossil of a "missing link," the animal that proves the relationship between one kind of animal and another.

What were man's earliest ancestors really like? What fossils lie hidden and waiting to be found by some future scientist?
ALSO READ: CELL; DARWIN, CHARLES; DINOSAUR; EARTH HISTORY; FOSSIL; GENETICS; MENDEL, GREGOR; PALEONTOLOGY; REPRODUCTION; WALLACE, ALFRED R.

EXERCISE   Any activity in which we use our muscles is exercise. But exercise usually means activities that strengthen the muscles and improve health. Group sports, such as baseball, football, basketball, volleyball, and hockey, are excellent ways to get exercise and have fun. So are individual sports such as swimming, gymnastics, cycling, or track. Social dancing, ballet, and modern dance all provide a chance for combining exercise with self-expression. Even taking walks every day is a good way to get exercise. It is better to have mild exercise often than to have strenuous exercise only once in a long while.

Some people do exercises called *calisthenics,* which are movements designed to strengthen specific muscles. *Isometrics* is a type of calisthenics in which muscles are strengthened by using them against each other or against an object that will not move, such as a wall or door frame. Would you like to try an isometric exercise? Raise your arms to shoulder height. Press the palms of your hands together. Press *hard.* If you're doing it correctly, you should feel the muscles in your arms and shoulders working.

Professional athletes do calisthenics to keep in shape. Calisthenics are also useful for people who do not have a chance to participate in sports. Many people like to exercise by *jogging*, running in easy strides for fairly long distances.

Exercise helps the blood to circulate through the muscle tissues, cleaning out waste and supplying more oxygen. The heart can then supply the body with blood more efficiently. Muscles become larger and better equipped to respond in an emergency as well as to handle everyday jobs. A good weight reduction program should include exercise as well as dieting. Regular exercise makes relaxation and sound, healthy sleep easier.

ALSO READ: CIRCULATORY SYSTEM, DANCING, GYMNASTICS, HEALTH, MUSCLE, PHYSICAL EDUCATION, SPORTS.

EXPLORATION   When an explorer was asked why he wished to climb Mount Everest, he replied, "Because it is there." When men *explore* they go where no other men have gone before, see what no other men have seen, and discover what no other men have ever before known.

Men like to explore for many reasons. They are curious and adventurous. Often they hope to come upon something that will make their lives easier or richer. Early cavemen ventured often into new territory in their constant search for food. Today, when men know where to find most of the material goods they need, their curiosity still leads them to want to explore the unknown. Exploration is still one of the great adventures available to man.

Early Exploration

We have no written records of early man's explorations, but historians know he must have been just as brave and imaginative as today's astronauts who explore outer space. In early times, man knew so much less about the world around him that every new step into strange lands seemed a dangerous adventure.

The first known discoverer who left records of his adventures was an Egyptian named Hannu in 2750 B.C. Hannu built a wooden ship and sailed south from Egypt along the Red Sea, then traveled over land to central Africa. He returned to Egypt in triumph with a cargo of monkeys, precious metals, incense, and tropical woods never before seen by his countrymen.

The first sea-going boats were so light and fragile that they could be sailed only in mild weather by day, and crews had to spend the night ashore. About 1,000 years before the birth of Christ, a remarkable people called the Phoenicians founded a nation at the eastern end of the Mediterranean. They used the strong wood from the great cedars of Lebanon, and built the first real long-range ships. The Phoenicians set out to discover and trade with all the other civilizations they could find. They established colonies as far away as England and may even have sailed around Africa.

The Greeks built a cultured and advanced civilization centuries before the birth of Christ. Some of the most adventurous Greek traders may have dared to travel very long distances out into the Atlantic Ocean. Alexander the Great, in the 330s and 320s B.C., explored and conquered all of the Middle East as far as India.

The Roman Empire was founded not so much by explorers as by mighty generals. The Romans extended their holdings to include most of Europe, the Middle East, and north Africa. After the Roman Empire was overrun by barbarian tribes, however, a period called the Middle Ages began. Few expeditions set out from Europe for the next thousand years.

The Middle Ages
Exploration continued in other parts of the world. Great empires existed in Africa, particularly in the western part. These empires were built up by imaginative explorers and maintained by lively caravan trade.

In Asia, too, there were probably a number of daring discoverers, although no known written history remains of their accomplishments. Most historians believe that the Indians of both North and South America came originally from Asia. Their ancestors must have been very brave explorers to risk crossing the icy wastes of Siberia and Alaska in search of warmer lands.

In Europe, the Vikings of Norway were the first to revive exploration. Recent discoveries in Newfoundland show that they had established an advanced colony there by about 1000 A.D., but abandoned it soon after.

Perhaps the most mysterious explorers were the Basques, a unique people that scholars believe are related to no other group of people in the world. The Basques now live in southern France and northern Spain. They claim they came originally from a continent called Atlantis, which has now sunk beneath the Atlantic Ocean. They may have discovered the Americas

Marco Polo sets out on his voyage to the mysterious east from Venice, Italy in 1271, as shown in a sixteenth-century miniature.

well before the Vikings, but they established no colonies, and they kept their discoveries a secret. Until Columbus sailed to the New World, most Europeans did not even suspect the Americas existed.

The Great Age of Exploration

By 1200 A.D., Europeans had begun looking around for ways to improve their lives. They heard that a mighty civilization existed in China—with a wealth of silks, jewels, and other treasures unknown in the West. Europeans knew that many spices grown in southern Asia could be used to preserve food. During the cold European winters, no fresh food was available.

A young Italian, Marco Polo, journeyed in caravans across Asia to China and became a close friend of the Emperor Kublai Khan. When Marco Polo returned to Europe, the story of his discoveries and of the wealth of the Orient created great interest in Asia. Growing trade between Europe and the East resulted. Ships sailed to the eastern end of the Mediterranean. Then traders traveled by caravan across Asia. Many cities of Italy soon became wealthy from this trade and gained control of the traffic in the Mediterranean Sea. Nations bordering on the Atlantic, particularly Portugal, were determined to find an alternate way to Asia to share in the riches.

Prince Henry of Portugal is known as "the discoverer of discoverers" because he encouraged explorers, and he promoted advances in ship construction and navigation. Under Henry's inspiration, Bartholomeu Dias sailed to the southern tip of Africa in 1488. Vasco da Gama followed Dias's route ten years later and continued on to India.

Christopher Columbus brought the startling news to Europe in 1492 that new lands lay to the west across the Atlantic. A host of followers explored the Americas. John Cabot was

▼Christopher Columbus and his men set foot on American soil in 1492. The great age of exploration of the New World had begun.

FAMOUS EXPLORERS

EXPLORER	BIRTHPLACE	AREA EXPLORED	DATE
Eric the Red	Norway	Discovered Greenland (s.w. coast).	982
Leif Ericson	Iceland	Probably the first European to reach North America.	1000
Marco Polo	Italy	Far East including India and China.	1271–95
Bartholomeu Dias	Portugal	First European to round the Cape of Good Hope.	1488
Christopher Columbus	Italy	Discovered America, opening the New World to all of Europe.	1492
John Cabot	Italy	East coast of Canada, and east and west coasts of Greenland. Discovered Newfoundland.	1497–98
Vasco da Gama	Portugal	First European to reach India by sea.	1498
Amerigo Vespucci	Italy	Made several voyages to the New World after Columbus. America was named after him.	1497–1503
Vasco Nunez de Balboa	Spain	Crossed Isthmus of Panama and discovered the Pacific Ocean.	1513
Ferdinand Magellan	Portugal	Commanded first voyage around the globe, sailing westward.	1519–21
Jacques Cartier	France	St. Lawrence River.	1534
Francisco Vasquez de Coronado	Spain	Traced Colorado River northward, discovering Grand Canyon. Explored southwestern states and eastern Kansas.	1540–42
Sir Francis Drake	England	First Englishman to sail around the world.	1577–80
Samuel de Champlain	France	Founded Quebec City and Lake Champlain.	1608–9
Henry Hudson	England	Hudson River, Bay, and Strait.	1609–11
Abel Janszoon Tasman	Holland	Discovered New Zealand and Tasmania.	1642
Vitus Bering	Denmark	Explored Bering Sea and Strait.	1728
James Cook	England	Explored and mapped South Pacific, including eastern coast of Australia.	1768–79
Alexander Mackenzie	Scotland	Discovered Mackenzie River and explored western Canada.	1789–93
Meriwether Lewis and William Clark	United States	Traveled over the Rocky Mountains to Pacific Ocean.	1804–6
David Livingstone	Scotland	Discovered Zambezi River and Victoria Falls and explored South Africa.	1849–73
Henry Stanley	Wales	Found correct source of the Nile River and explored Congo River region.	1874–89
Robert Peary	United States	Led first expedition to North Pole.	1908–9
Roald Amundsen	Norway	First to reach South Pole. Flew over North Pole in a dirigible airship with Nobile & Ellsworth	1911 1926
Richard E. Byrd	United States	First man to fly over North Pole.	1926
Bertram Thomas	England	First European to cross the great desert, the Rub' al Khali, in southern Arabia.	1930–31
Edmund Hillary	New Zealand	First to reach the summit of Mount Everest, on border of Nepal and Tibet.	1953
Yuri Gargarin	Soviet Union	First man in space.	1961
Neil Armstrong and Edwin Aldrin	United States	First men to explore the moon.	1969

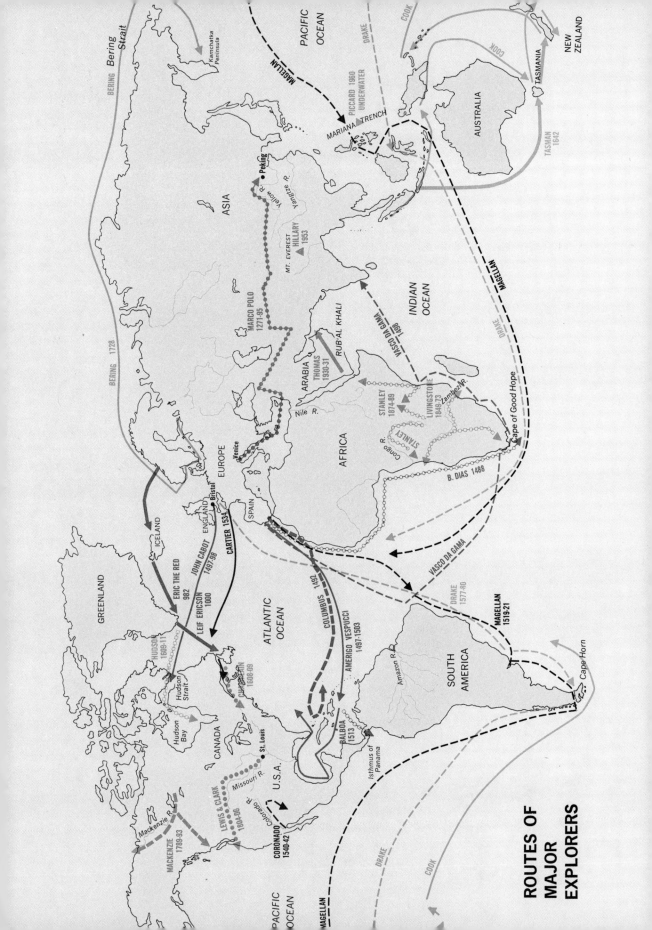

ROUTES OF MAJOR EXPLORERS

the first to reach what is now Canada, and Jacques Cartier came soon afterwards, exploring the St. Lawrence. Giovanni de Verrazano, Captain John Smith, Sir Walter Raleigh, and Henry Hudson soon traveled throughout the eastern seaboard of what is now the United States.

The French explorers, Louis Joliet and Jacques Marquette, discovered the headwaters of the Mississippi, and Sieur de La Salle explored that river to its mouth. Antoine Cadillac founded Detroit and was governor of Louisiana. Hernando de Soto was the first to penetrate what is now the southern U.S. But it was the black adventurer, Estevanico, who discovered the vast lands of what would become Texas and Arizona. His explorations paved the way for Francisco Coronado's discoveries in the southwestern U.S.

In 1513, Vasco Balboa crossed Panama and discovered that the Pacific Ocean lay beyond. Many people still believed that Asia could not be far away. Between 1519 and 1521, Ferdinand Magellan led an expedition that sailed around the world. For the first time, the real size of the world—particularly the large size of the Americas and the Pacific—was realized. Magellan's expedition took three long and desperate years to circumnavigate the globe. Astronauts now fly around the Earth in little more than 90 minutes!

Sir Francis Drake followed the route that Magellan's ships had sailed. Captain James Cook continued the exploration of the South Pacific. In the North, the Danish explorer, Vitus Bering, mapped the treacherous reaches of the Siberian Arctic and Alaska.

Modern Exploration

The coldest parts of the world, the Arctic and Antarctic, were not explored until the 1900s. Rear Admiral Robert Peary of the U.S. Navy, traveling by dog team, reached the North Pole in 1909. In 1958, the U.S. nuclear submarine *Nautilus* sailed across the Arctic Ocean entirely under the water and passed beneath the pole, 400 feet under the ice. Roald Amundsen, a Norwegian explorer, beat an Englishman, Robert Scott, in a race to the South Pole in 1911.

The age of exploration is not over. Indeed, in many areas it is just beginning. The depths of the ocean still hold many challenges for man. In 1960, Jacques Piccard and U.S. Navy Lieutenant Donald Walsh descended almost seven miles to the bottom of the Pacific in a pressurized capsule called a *bathyscaph.* And the peaks of many mountains remain to be conquered. The world's highest peak, Mount Everest, is almost 6 miles high and required 11 attempts before Edmund Hillary and Tensing Norkay reached the summit in 1953. The mystery and challenge of the Earth's interior also remains to be explored. The science-

▼*In 1969, the S.S.* Manhattan, *an American tanker, and the* John A. Macdonald, *a Canadian ice-breaker, explored the Northwest Passage. The* Manhattan *was the first commercial ship to conquer the passage.*

fiction writer Jules Verne suggested that the Earth was hollow. Man does not know what he will discover more than seven miles below the Earth's surface.

Space Exploration

Space is perhaps the most exciting challenge for explorers. When the American astronaut Neil Armstrong became the first human to set foot on the surface of the moon, he declared "That's one small step for a man, one giant leap for mankind."

Similar giant steps await mankind throughout the universe. Suspense mounts as scientists study the planet Mars. Man's first step on the planet Mars may not be very far away. Whether or not Mars has some form of life, the odds seem overwhelming that somewhere among the billions of other heavenly bodies in the universe, some form of life must exist. The discoveries of the next century will probably make the mighty explorations of all past ages seem minor by comparison. The possibilities for discovery that await a brave explorer seem unlimited.

For further information on:

Explorers, *see* BALBOA, VASCO NUNEZ DE; BERING, VITUS; CABOT, JOHN AND SEBASTIAN; CADILLAC, ANTOINE; CARTIER, JACQUES; COLUMBUS, CHRISTOPHER; COOK, CAPTAIN J.; CORONADO, FRANCISCO; DE SOTO, HERNANDO; DIAS, BARTHOLOMEU; DRAKE, SIR FRANCIS; ESTEVANICO; GAMA, VASCO DA; HILLARY, EDMUND; HUDSON, HENRY; JOLIET AND MARQUETTE; LA SALLE, SIEUR DE; MAGELLAN, FERDINAND; PEARY, ROBERT; POLO, MARCO; RALEIGH, SIR WALTER; SMITH, CAPTAIN JOHN; STANLEY, HENRY MORTON; VERRAZANO, GIOVANNI DA; VIKINGS.

Geography, *see* AFRICA, ANTARCTICA, ARCTIC, ASIA, ATLANTIC OCEAN, HIMALAYA MOUNTAINS, NORTH AMERICA, NORTH POLE, NORTHWEST PASSAGE, OCEAN, PACIFIC OCEAN, SOUTH AMERICA, SOUTH POLE.

History, *see* ALEXANDER THE GREAT; ATLANTIS; CARTHAGE; CHINA; CRUSADES; EGYPT, ANCIENT; GREECE, ANCIENT; HENRY THE NAVIGATOR; INDIANS, AMERICAN; NAVIGATION; PHOENICIA; ROMAN EMPIRE; SHIPS AND SHIPPING.

Space Exploration, *see* APOLLO; ARMSTRONG, NEIL; ASTRONAUT; MOON; SPACE; SPACE TRAVEL.

▲ *A drawing of an orbiting space station designed to house between 50 and 100 people. See the space shuttle vehicles docked at the lower portion of the station. Orbiting space stations will be used in future exploration of the solar system.*

EXPLOSIVES A pioneer farmer would spend a whole morning chopping away a large tree stump. Today, a farmer takes five minutes to shatter a stump with an explosive.

An explosive is a substance that very quickly—in a few millionths of a second—produces a great amount of energy in the form of heat and expanding gas. The gas expands to a volume hundreds of times as big as the explosive. The gas travels outward at a very high speed from where the explosion has oc-

►*Explosives destroy Ripple Rock, a navigational hazard located in Seymour Narrows, British Columbia. Demolition squads used almost three million pounds of a nitrogen-base blasting agent in the explosion.*

curred. It is this high-speed, expanding volume of gas that causes explosives to have so much force.

Explosives are used in almost all weapons of modern warfare. Many kinds of explosives are used in peaceful activities, such as blasting rock mines, building roads and dams, and breaking up ice jams in rivers.

Kinds of Explosives

The three main types of explosives are mechanical, chemical, and nuclear. One kind of *mechanical* explosive is called *cardox.* Cardox consists of a sealed metal tube filled with liquid carbon dioxide and a means of heating the tube. Heat causes the liquid to become a gas that bursts the seal and expands rapidly. Cardox is a slow, low-powered explosive used in mines to split and heave rock, rather than shatter it.

The two kinds of *chemical* explosives are the low and high explosives. A *low explosive* burns very rapidly after it is set afire. It explodes only when enclosed in a strong container. Otherwise, it simply burns in a flash. A large amount of gas results from burning a low explosive. This gas produces waves of very high pressure, within the container, finally bursting it and making an explosion. *Gunpowder* is a low explosive used to push bullets and shells out of guns, and for making fireworks.

A *high explosive* is one in which heat and gas are produced by a very fast chemical reaction. This reaction may be started by a shock caused by striking the explosive. Or it may be started by the shock of a small explosion in a device that is very sensitive to heat or impact, called a *detonator.* Blasting caps are detonators that explode and then cause dynamite to explode. Sometimes workmen carelessly leave behind unused blasting caps when they finish their blasting. If you should ever find a blasting cap, do not touch it with anything because it can be very dangerous. Call a policeman or fireman to remove it safely.

High explosives generally expand faster and are more powerful than low explosives, so they are used where great shattering force is needed, as in bombs. High explosives cannot be used in guns. The suddenness with which high explosives explode would blow a gun apart before a bullet could shoot out.

Nuclear explosives depend on the immense amount of heat—millions of degrees—that is produced by either *nuclear fission* or *nuclear fusion.* The heat expands the surrounding air with extreme speed, giving it explosive force. Nuclear explosives are the most powerful known. The *atomic bomb* explodes by fission, and the *hydrogen bomb* by fusion.

History

Historians say the Chinese invented gunpowder, which they used in fireworks, in the 800s A.D. The English scientist, Roger Bacon, wrote a formula for making gunpowder in the 1200s. It was first used in guns in the 1300s. Nitroglycerin was discovered in 1846, but it was so highly explosive that it was not used much. Then, in 1867, the Swedish chemist, Alfred Nobel, discovered that nitroglycerin could be safely used if mixed with a type of earth called kieselguhr. Nobel called the mixture dynamite. The powerful high explosive TNT was invented in Germany and used in both world wars. During World War II, even more powerful explosives—including the atomic bomb—were developed and used.

ALSO READ: CHEMISTRY, FIREWORKS, GAS, GUNS AND RIFLES, MINES AND MINING, NUCLEAR ENERGY.

EXPRESSIONISM   Have you ever gone somewhere you had often been to before and found it looked very different? Your favorite playground, where you and your friends have exciting times, might seem like a bright place with yellow slides and whizzing red merry-go-rounds. Go there alone early some Sunday morning, and it might look dark and gloomy gray, a strangely different place. Your feelings "color" the way a place looks to you and colors themselves can bring out feelings—gray for gloom, blue for sadness, red for anger, and so on.

Feelings also color the way *expressionist* artists paint. See the expressionist painting shown here. It's called *Anxiety,* which means "worry" or "concern." You could probably tell, even without knowing the title, that the people in this painting are unhappy. Edvard Munch (1863–1944), the artist, chose dark, sad blues and violets to express his feeling of fear. See the big, sad eyes of the woman. Notice her pale greenish skin and

▼Anxiety, *an expressionist painting by the Norwegian artist Edvard Munch.*

her down-turned mouth. The men have faces like skulls or *death's heads*. The black, stiff clothes remind you of death.

The most disturbing fact is that you don't know why these people are all so worried. Munch doesn't give a clue. Did someone die? Is someone lost? Has a bomb struck? You will never know.

Edvard Munch, one of the first and greatest expressionists, was born in Norway. He studied painting in France, but he spent most of his career in Germany. Munch's manner of expressing his feelings about a place or subject in colors and composition influenced other painters very much. Many German and other northern painters became expressionists, too.

The expressionists felt strongly about poverty, suffering, and violence. They felt that it was being honest to paint these subjects, since most of the painters themselves were poor, suffering, or feeling violent. Some expressionists even said that an artist who painted a beautiful scene of a sunny day with all the people smiling contentedly was not telling the truth about life.

Some expressionists wanted to shock people—to end the tradition of painting everything prettier than real life. People were shocked by the expressionists, and many became angry. For hundreds of years, artists had used *caricatures* (cartoons) to exaggerate, or enlarge, any unusual features a person had. An artist could draw a cartoon of a person whose nose was big by drawing the nose extra large. People could laugh at this. Caricatures were meant to be funny, but the expressionists exaggerated very seriously—making life sadder and uglier than it is.

When Adolf Hitler and his National Socialists came to power in Germany, German expressionists were forbidden to paint. Many of these artists left the country. Expressionism spread to France, England, the United States, and other countries that provided political freedom.

ALSO READ: GAUGUIN, PAUL; IMPRESSIONISM; MODERN ART; VAN GOGH, VINCENT.

EXTRASENSORY PERCEPTION Did you ever feel that you knew what a person was going to say just before he said it? You did not simply have a vague idea that he was going to say it, but you *knew* it. Perhaps you only made a very clever guess. Perhaps you made use of *extrasensory perception* to read his mind.

Extra here means "outside of." *Sensory* means "of the senses,"* which are sight, hearing, smell, touch, and taste. *Perception* means "being aware of." So extrasensory perception is being aware of something by means outside your senses. You felt you knew what someone was going to say, although there was no way your senses could tell you. Extrasensory perception is often abbreviated ESP.

Ever since ancient times, certain people have claimed extrasensory abilities. Some believed they knew the future, and they told fortunes. Others thought they could talk with ghosts and spirits. Still others said they could read minds. A group of men met in London in 1882 and formed the Society for Psychical Research. They set out to apply science in investigating claims of extrasensory perception. Since then, others have tried to do the same thing. No one has ever found the claims to be altogether true, but research into ESP continues.

Dr. J. B. Rhine of Duke University set up a research program into ESP in 1930. He and his co-workers have done much work on *telepathy*. This is the ability to read a person's mind or to send another person thoughts, without a word being said. The ESP researchers have used a deck of 25 cards with certain symbols, or signs, on them. Dr. Rhine has claimed that many persons can tell what is on the cards even though these persons cannot see them. He says that the scores they make in telling what is on the cards are better than they would make if they were just guessing. Other researchers say that Dr. Rhine's experiments are not done scientifically, and therefore, his results do not prove that ESP exists.

You can conduct your own experiments on ESP. First, try flipping a coin. Can you tell before the coin lands whether it will be "heads" or "tails?" If you flip the coin 100 times, the *laws of chance* say that you should have the right answer half the time, or on 50 tosses. If you answer right 60 or 70 times, perhaps you have had a little help from ESP.

Now try an experiment with a friend. Sit with your back to him. Have him flip the coin 100 times, and, each time it lands, have him *think* whether it landed "heads" or "tails." After each toss, he should write down how the coin landed, and you should write down how you think it landed. Compare notes after the last toss. Again, according to the laws of chance, you should be right about half the time. How did you do? What do *you* think of ESP?

ALSO READ: CHANCE AND PROBABILITY, PSYCHOLOGY.

▲*An electronic machine is used to discover whether a girl has ESP. The girl tries to guess which of four colored lamps will next light. A high number of correct guesses indicated she has ESP.*

EYE   The eye is the organ of sight. Some animals have simple eyes, which can only "see" changes in brightness. Other animals have more highly developed eyes, which can see shapes, movement, and color. One of the most complex eyes of all is man's. Your eyes give you much more information about the world around you than all of your other senses together.

Parts of the Eye
The outside, transparent, protective layer of the eye is called the *cornea*. The *iris* lies behind it. This is a colored screen—blue, brown, gray, or a variation of these colors. The dark center is

▶ *A cross-section of the hu-man eye.*

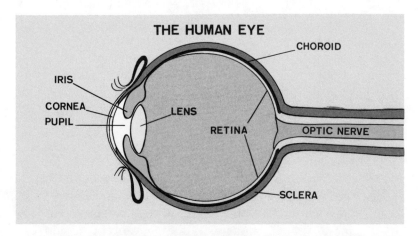

▶ A cross-section of the human eye.

THE HUMAN EYE

called the *pupil*. This dark circle opens up in the dark to let in more light. It narrows in bright sunlight to reduce the amount of light entering the eye. This adjustment helps people see as much as possible under different light conditions.

You and a friend can see the pupil at work. Have your friend stand facing a bright light. You stand in front of him and facing him, but do not stand so that you block the light. Your friend should cover his eyes with his hands and count slowly to 25. He then should remove his hands quickly. Watch his eyes carefully as he does this. Change places and do the same thing. What did each of you see? What causes this?

The *lens* of the eye lies behind the pupil. It is a crystalline, transparent disc, thick in the middle and thin at the edges. It is about one-third of an inch in diameter. The central part of the lens is suspended by ligaments a little distance behind the pupil. Its function is to focus the light onto a screen that lines the back of the eyeball, the *retina*.

The retina consists of cells that are sensitive to light. It is made up of two types of cells called *rods* and *cones*. When light strikes the retina, impulses are set up and transmitted by the nerves to the visual areas of the brain.

The cones perceive color and work best in good light. They respond to much stronger light than the rods. They enable us to see objects in finer detail. The rods, on the other hand, are not sensitive to color—only black and white. They make it possible to see in dim light. When we work in a dim light, we tend to see things in tones of gray. Have you noticed, for instance, that the colors of a landscape seem to fade at twilight?

How the Eye Works

The eye works like a camera in many ways. Both focus light through a lens onto a screen to get a picture. The shutter in the camera is like the pupil in the eye. We open up a camera shutter to allow more light to reach the film on a gray day. On a sunny day, you close the shutter—making it a tiny hole—to stop much light from striking the film when you trip the shutter of the camera.

When you use a complicated camera, you focus the picture you wish to throw on the film by moving the lens back and forth. Focusing in the human eye is done by changes in the shape of the lens. It lets you see objects that are far away or very near with the same lens.

Muscles attached to the lens alter the lens's shape. When you look at a distant object, the lens muscles are relaxed. But when you want to read small print, the muscles tense up and make the lens thicker. This brings the object into focus. You can find the near focal point of your vision by gradually moving a pencil toward your eyes and locating the distance at which it becomes blurred and your eyes cannot bring it into focus.

▲*Cats have good eyesight in the dark because in dim light the narrow irises of their eyes grow rounder and allow more light to enter. They cannot see in total darkness.*

Common Problems with Eyesight

One of the most familiar problems with being able to see is being *nearsighted.* This condition happens when the eyeball is very long or the cornea is too curved, so that the lens cannot focus on the retina for faraway objects. Other people have trouble seeing objects that are close. They are *farsighted.* The eyeball is too short or the cornea is not curved enough. This is often a problem of people over age 40. They need glasses for reading. Still another problem is *astigmatism,* caused by having an unevenly curved cornea. This causes blurred vision. Wearing glasses can correct these problems. The way an animal lives usually determines what kind of vision it has. Animals that fly or climb or eat other animals need better vision than those who live underground or eat plants. Some invertebrate animals have eyes like those of man, and others have compound eyes. A compound eye is made up of small units or long cylinders called omnatidia. A tiny part of an object is seen on each cylinder and put together like a mosaic picture.

ALSO READ: CAMERA, COLOR BLINDNESS, DIMENSION, SENSE ORGAN, SIGHT.

◄*A red-tailed hawk with its eyes open* (left). *The same hawk with its inner eyelid closed* (right). *All birds have this protective membrane.*

FABLE "Think twice before you act." "Laziness is its own punishment." Each of these sentences is the moral of a story. A *moral* is a bit of advice about how to live, or a truth about life. Morals are often taught by short stories called fables. Many fables have animal characters who behave like people. Some fables are poems.

"Think twice before you act" is the moral of a fable about two frogs. One frog wanted to jump into a well because the water looked so clear and inviting. But the other frog was afraid to jump. He was worried about how they would get out if the well dried up. Do you think he was wise?

"Laziness is its own punishment" is the moral of a fable about two maids. A crowing rooster woke them early each morning. The maids killed the rooster so that they could sleep later. But from then on their mistress woke them up every morning. And she woke them even earlier than the rooster had.

Fables have been told for thousands of years. They were passed on by word of mouth from generation to generation. One of the great tellers of fables was Aesop. Legend says he was a slave who lived in Greece in the sixth century B.C. His fables were not written down until about 200 years after his death.

A sly creature called Reynard the Fox was the clever hero of countless fables written in Europe during the Middle Ages. One of the greatest fable-tellers of all time was Jean de la Fontaine, a Frenchman. He published many books of fables in the seventeenth century. His fables are still famous all over the world. La Fontaine influenced many other writers. Hans Christian Andersen, the Danish author, used the fable idea in several of his fairy tales. The American writers George Ade, James Thurber, and William Saroyan have also written entertaining books of fables. Even some of Walt Disney's cartoon movies tell stories similar to fables.

Do you think you could write a fable? Think of a saying, like "absence makes the heart grow fonder"; "out of sight, out of mind"; "a stitch in time saves nine"; or "he who hesitates is lost." Can you think of any situation that proves that one of these sayings is true? Make up characters, either animals or people, and give them things to say and do that prove your moral is true.

ALSO READ: AESOP; ANDERSEN, HANS CHRISTIAN; LA FONTAINE, JEAN DE.

▲*Jean de la Fontaine's fable "The Fox and the Crow" tells of a fox that sees a crow perched on a tree with some cheese in its beak. The fox slyly asks the crow to sing. As soon as the crow begins to caw, the cheese falls from its beak and is eaten by the fox. The crow learned an important lesson—not to trust flatterers.*

FABRE, J. HENRI (1823-1915) Have you ever been amazed as you watched ants struggle to bring a huge piece of food back to their nest? Have you ever been fascinated by the engineering that a spider must do to build its web? If so, you have shared a feeling of wonder with Henri Fabre, a great *entomologist* (a scientist who studies insects). Fabre was one of the first men ever to study living insects, rather than the dead, mounted specimens in a museum collection.

Jean Henri Casimir Fabre came from a very poor family. He worked to pay for his studies at the University of Paris and then became a teacher of chemistry and physics. He read a book on insects at the same time he started teaching. Fabre became so interested in insects that he studied them for the rest of his life.

In 1870, he was dismissed from his teaching post for admitting girls to his classes. For the next nine years, Fabre supported himself by writing, explaining science to children.

Fabre spent the last third of his life observing and writing about insects and spiders. He studied these creatures in the field and did experiments with them in his laboratory. His books on his work are still read by people interested in nature.

ALSO READ: INSECT, SPIDER.

▲County and state agricultural fairs are important events in the U.S. Farmers exhibit and sell their animals. Prizes are awarded for outstanding achievements.

FAIR A fair is an event to which many people come to buy, sell, or show goods. The earliest fairs took place at times when large groups of people gathered to celebrate religious festivals. Farmers and craftsmen would bring their goods and display them. Such fairs were held in ancient Greece, Rome, and China. Similar fairs were held throughout Europe during the Middle Ages. Kings also gave certain cities special permission to have fairs. The region of Champagne in France became well known for its fairs, which featured goods such as furs from Russia, cloth from England, and spices from Asia. Other great fairs were held in Brussels in Belgium, Leipzig in Germany, and Stourbridge in England. A special fair just for showing horses was held each year in Nizhni Novgorod (now Gorky) in Russia. The Bartholomew Fair in London, England—held in honor of Saint Bartholomew around his feast day on August 24—was the first fair known for its plays and other amusements, rather than for its trade exhibits. It was first held during the 1100s.

Fairs in the United States

County and state fairs are usually held once a year in the U.S. Those in colonial days were rather simple. Farmers gathered to buy and sell seeds, livestock, and farming tools. Fairs in the 1800s began also to feature demonstrations of better methods of raising crops and breeding livestock. Other communities later added contests for the best fruits and vegetables, the finest handmade quilts, and the tastiest homemade jams, jellies, pies, and cakes. Prizes were also given for the best cows, pigs, and other farm animals. County and state fairs today often exhibit the latest farming equipment and provide amusement areas with rides, games, sideshows, races, and refreshment stands. Sometimes shows are performed featuring famous entertainers.

World's Fairs

Another kind of fair is the exposition or world's fair. These fairs attract people from all over the world, and many nations

▶The Great Exhibition, opened by Queen Victoria in 1851, was one of the world's first big international fairs. Over six million people saw more than 15,000 exhibits housed in a beautiful glass and iron building, the Crystal Palace.

◀Expo 67 took place in Montreal, Canada, in 1967. Seventy-six nations took part to display their successes in industry, science, and the arts. The Russian Pavilion is in the foreground and the American Pavilion is in the background.

take part in them. The exhibits demonstrate new ideas and achievements in industry, farming, science, and the arts. One of the first great world's fairs was held in London, England, in the Crystal Palace in 1851. The Crystal Palace, a magnificent building of glass and iron, was especially constructed for the fair. Many people thought the building was as wonderful as the exhibits inside it. The United States sent 560 exhibits there, including Cyrus McCormick's grain reaper and a display of false teeth and artificial legs.

Other countries soon began to hold similar expositions. The Centennial Exposition, held in Philadelphia in 1876, celebrated the one-hundredth anniversary of U.S. independence. Recent inventions of that time, such as the telephone and the typewriter, were shown. Chicago was the site of the World's Columbian Exposition in 1893. It celebrated the four-hundredth anniversary of Columbus's discovery of America. People who visited this exposition marveled at demonstrations of the latest developments in electricity. Many also took a thrilling ride on the first Ferris wheel, which had been built especially for the occasion. Other famous international expositions have been the 1958 World's Fair in Brussels, Belgium; the New York World's Fair of 1964–1965; and Expo 67 in Montreal, Canada. Expo 70, the first world's fair ever held in Asia, took place in Osaka, Japan.

World's fairs require long and careful planning. Preparations for the international exposition of 1967—held in Montreal, Canada, involved the work of many engineers, artists, writers, and other professionals, and began several years in advance. The nations that participate in world's fairs also spend millions of dollars to make their exhibits attractive and interesting to the public.

The structures built for many fairs continue to attract visitors long after the fair ends. The Eiffel Tower, for example, was built for the Paris Exposition of 1893. Today it is the most famous landmark of the French capital. The tower also had an important influence on the development of modern skyscrapers.

Have a Fair

Gather some friends together to plan a fair. Decide where you can have it—perhaps in someone's back yard or a nearby park. Think up games everyone can play. Maybe some people can bake cookies or make lemonade to sell. Can someone pretend to be a fortune-teller? How about including a pet show, a play, or exhibits of things friends have created? Make posters to advertise the fair, telling where and when it will be held and some of the wonderful things people will see.

ALSO READ: CARNIVAL, CIRCUS, RODEO.

FAIRY TALE   A story may be a journey into another kind of world, a magic visit to the land of make-believe. Fairy tales often begin with the words "Once upon a time. . . ." They take place in faraway, imaginary places where unusual events occur as if they were ordinary happenings. Long ago, when few people owned books, stories were passed down from generation to generation by word of mouth. Some of the tales were based on folklore, or the traditions of a group of people. Many of these stories, especially those for children, were written down and became the familiar fairy tales.

All fairy tales share certain features. Fairies, elves, leprechauns, trolls, brownies, and pixies are often important characters. But these imaginary creatures need not always be included. Animals—both real and imaginary—may be in the story, too. Sometimes they can talk the way people do. Kings, queens, handsome princes, and beautiful princesses also take part.

Fairy tales may tell about an imaginary person's life and how the forces of good and evil challenge one another during his lifetime. For example, a wicked witch may cast a spell that turns a little boy into a mushroom. Then, with the help of a kind fairy, the spell at last is broken. At the end of the tale, everything works out for the good characters, and the story ends with "they lived happily ever after."

In many stories, the number 3 is important. The main character may make three guesses, take three tries, or have three wishes. In other stories, there are three brothers or three sisters. Can you think of any other "threes" in fairy tales?

Some Famous Fairy Tales

One of the earliest collections of actual fairy tales appeared in 1697. A Frenchman, Charles Perrault, published a group of eight charming stories, called *Mother Goose's Fairy Tales.*

One of Perrault's stories was "The Sleeping Beauty," the story of a princess. All of the fairies in the kingdom were invited

▼*A scene from "Puss in Boots," a fairy tale by the brothers Grimm. Puss meets all kinds of people in an effort to make a fortune for his master.*

to a great banquet to present gifts to the baby princess. One aged fairy was forgotten, as she lived in a tower and had not been seen for many years. The old fairy was so angry that she appeared at the banquet to say that the little princess would one day prick her finger on a spindle (part of a spinning wheel) and die. One of the good fairies changed the spell so that the princess would not die, but only sleep for 100 years. She was awakened by a young prince, who fought his way through brambles and thorns to claim the princess with a kiss. The much-told tale of Cinderella and her glass slipper was another Perrault story, and so were "Bluebeard" and "Little Red Riding Hood."

▲"Tom Thumb" is a Grimm fairy tale about the adventures of a tiny man. Here he is riding a horse that is far too big for him.

The brothers Jakob and Wilhelm Grimm, who lived in Germany in the early 1800s, collected many folk tales. Their book, *Grimm's Fairy Tales,* is famous all over the world. "Hansel and Gretel," "Snow White," and "Rumpelstiltskin" are among the stories they collected. Hans Christian Andersen of Denmark wrote many wonderful fairy tales. The amusing "Princess and the Pea," the sad "Little Match Girl," and the beloved "Ugly Duckling" are a few of his most famous stories. Andrew Lang was a Scottish scholar who searched far and wide for fairy tales. He published his finds in a series of books called the Blue, Red, Green, and Yellow Fairy Books. Thomas Crofton Croker's book of Irish fairy tales is another well-known, excellent collection. George Macdonald wrote several enchanting books about a boy named Curdie and his adventures with goblins, but his best-known book is *At the Back of the North Wind.*

The Study of Fairy Tales

When the Grimm brothers published their collection of fairy tales, other writers began to think of the folk tales of their own countries. They discovered that many of the stories from different parts of the world are very much alike. Some scholars think that all folk tales originally came from one source, perhaps the peoples of northern Europe. Others feel that fairy tales began in India and were carried all over the world by merchants and wandering tribes.

Find a book of fairy tales in the library. When you have finished reading the stories, choose the one you like the best. Act out the story with a group of your friends or members of your family. If you prefer, make up your own fairy tale to act out. Try to find a few costumes and props around the house. An old torn sheet might be just the right ball gown for a princess. Hats and crowns can be made with newspaper, crayons, and tape. What would you make fairy's wings from? An old, large box can be cut up into shields or wands. Or leave the box whole and make it part of the scenery. A packing crate could be a castle or a dragon's cave.

FALCONRY

After all the actors have learned their lines, and the costumes and scenery are ready, it is time to present your play. Invite family members, neighbors, and friends to be your audience.

ALSO READ: ANDERSEN, HANS CHRISTIAN; ARABIAN NIGHTS; CHILDREN'S LITERATURE; ELVES AND FAIRIES; GENIE; GRIMM BROTHERS; MOTHER GOOSE; PERRAULT, CHARLES.

FALCONRY Ever since ancient times men have trained falcons to hunt other birds and small animals. The sport of hunting with these birds is called hawking, or falconry.

Various types of falcons are used for hunting different types of quarry. All falcons belong to a group with the Latin name *Falco,* but in addition, some members of *Falco* are called "hawks" in English. Hawks are also found in other Latin-named groups. All hawks are powerful, fast fliers. They have strong legs and long toes tipped with sharp claws that grasp and hold the prey. Their sharp, hooked beaks help to kill the prey. Among the types of birds and animals hunted by falcons are wild ducks, pigeons, partridges, geese, rabbits, and hares.

People who train and hunt with falcons are called *falconers.* The bird must be trained to sit quietly on the falconer's arm. The falconer wears a heavy leather glove called a *gauntlet* to protect his arm. Then the bird must learn to wear a hood that covers its eyes. The hood keeps it quiet. The falconer walks through fields until he spots some prey. Then he pulls the hood off the bird's head. The bird sights the prey, darts to it, and kills it. Some birds only grasp the prey and hold it tightly, but unharmed, until the falconer comes for it.

A hawk taken from the nest when young is called an *eyas.* A captured wild hawk is a *hawk of passage.* Hawks of passage are harder to train, but they are better fliers and hunters than eyas.

Falconry as a sport originated in China before 2000 B.C., and was practiced in Japan, India, and other Asian countries as early as 600 B.C. Many ancient Egyptian wall paintings show the sport of falconry. The Romans introduced the sport to Europe. Falconry later became extremely popular in England. In fact, during the Middle Ages, the type of hawk an English nobleman carried on his wrist indicated his rank!

Falconry is practiced in nearly every part of the world today, from North Africa to the Netherlands to the United States. Although it is still a popular sport, the popularity of falconry declined with the invention of firearms.

ALSO READ: BIRDS OF PREY, HUNTING, SPORTS.

▲ *A falcon perched on the gauntlet of its trainer. The hood placed over the bird's eyes keeps it quiet until it is released to make a kill.*

FAMOUS ALPHABET An amusing game requiring a little concentration is Famous Alphabet. You will need pencils and paper for each player. Any number of persons can play. Each player writes down the letters of the alphabet in a column on his paper. One player chooses a letter, such as B. The letter B will be the *first letter of the last name* of all the famous people the players think up. A time limit of from 20 to 30 minutes is set, and the players begin. They must write down, beginning with the letter A on their paper, the name of a famous person whose first name begins with A and whose last name begins with B, such as *A*lexander *B*ell—the man who invented the telephone. The next letter on their list is B, so they must think up a name of someone whose first name begins *and* ends with B— *B*ugs *B*unny, for instance. The next letter on the list is C. *C*lara *B*arton could be used for this one. At the end of thirty minutes, the person with the most famous names on his list is the winner.

FARADAY, MICHAEL (1791-1867) Michael Faraday is famous for his work in chemistry and physics. He was born in London. His family was too poor to keep him in school, so he started working for a bookseller at age 13. He read the books he handled every day, and he attended science lectures at night. Before long, he became a laboratory assistant to Sir Humphry Davy, one of the most famous scientists of that time. Faraday learned much from this good teacher.

Faraday's most important discovery was that electricity can be produced by magnetism in motion. The invention of electric motors and generators was made possible by this discovery. The basic laws of electromagnetism, electrochemistry (the studies of electricity and chemistry combined), and electrometallurgy (using electricity to affect metals) were set forth by Faraday. His experiments led him to the idea that all space is "filled" with lines of force—gravitational, magnetic, electric, and thermal (heat). Other physicists developed Faraday's ideas, making possible the theories of Einstein and a revolution in physics.

The *farad,* a unit of electrical measurement, is named for Faraday. And the two basic laws of electrolysis (causing chemical changes or destruction of living tissue through the use of an electric current) are known as Faraday's Laws.

ALSO READ: CHEMISTRY, ELECTRICITY, ELECTRIC POWER, PHYSICS.

FARM MACHINERY Farmers once had few tools to help them, and they had to work hard to grow enough food for their families. But many kinds of farm machinery have been invented to make their work easier. These inventions made it possible for farmers to feed many people—to grow vast fields of crops or to raise huge herds of livestock.

The *plow* is one of the farmer's oldest pieces of machinery. It digs up the earth before the seeds are planted. Farmers were greatly aided by the cast-iron plow, patented by Charles New-

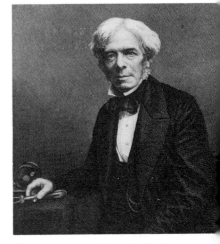

▲*Michael Faraday, English scientist.*

For many years Michael Faraday gave science lectures especially for children. One of the best lectures is called "The Chemical History of a Candle." See if your library has this wonderful story.

▼*A tractor-pulled plow cuts up the soil before seeds are planted.*

bold in 1797. It did not wear out like earlier plows made of soft metals. Today a plow with four or more blades is hitched to a *tractor,* the farmer's most useful machine. The farmer drives the tractor through the field, and the plow is dragged behind it. A tractor-pulled plow can dig a wide, long strip of soil in a very short time.

When the plowing is finished, the soil is rough. Other machines, called *harrows,* are hauled by the tractor to smooth out the dirt. After the harrowing, seeds are planted by an *automatic planter.* This machine, also pulled by the tractor, has several containers filled with seed. It also has containers carrying dry or liquid fertilizer. As the machine moves, it drops the seed and fertilizer together into rows. The seeds are covered, and the planting is completed.

As the crop grows, it needs care. Weeds must be removed, and the soil must be kept soft. A machine called a *cultivator* does this job. The farmer's tractor pulls the cultivator through the field. As the tractor moves, the cultivator loosens the earth and destroys weeds. A farmer may use other machines during the growing season. These include sprayers for insecticides, fertilizer distributors, and ditch diggers.

Crops used to be harvested by hand. The first grain harvesting machine used in the U.S. was invented by Cyrus McCormick in 1831. It was called a *reaper* and was pulled by a horse. Today farmers use different machines to do this job. One is a *combine,* which performs several harvesting operations. It harvests wheat, oats, and other grains. Part of the combine, the *thresher,* removes the grain from the straw. It separates and cleans the grain to be stored. If the crop is hay, the farmer may use an automatic *baler.* This machine picks up hay that has been cut, and gathers it into big square or oblong bales, tied with heavy cord. If the crop is corn, a *corn picker* is used to pick the ears from the plants.

A farmer usually hires a team of men who own combines to harvest his crops. Combine owners start their work in the mid-summer by harvesting the winter wheat in the south-central United States. They move northward, all the way to

▼*An interseeder* (below) *is a type of automatic planter used for seeding. A combine* (right) *cuts, threshes, and cleans grain.*

An automatic baler (left) *picks up hay that has been cut and packs it into big oblong bales. Animal fodder* (above) *is here conveyed from a harvester to a blower. The blower fans the fodder into a silo for storage.*

Canada, to harvest the spring wheat and other grains that ripen later in the summer and early fall.

Many other machines also help the farmer do his work more quickly. Farmers who raise animals also use machinery. For example, a poultry farmer may feed his turkeys automatically. He presses a button on a control panel to mix and grind the corn and other foods. Compressed air blows the feed through pipes into different feeding troughs where the turkeys eat. And the dairy farmer uses electric machines for milking cows. As you read the articles listed below, you can learn more about farm machines.

ALSO READ: AGRICULTURE; CATTLE; COTTON; DAIRY FARMING; FRUIT; GRAIN; MC CORMICK, CYRUS; POULTRY; RICE; TOBACCO; WHEAT; WHITNEY, ELI.

FARRAGUT, DAVID (1801–1870) "Damn the torpedoes! Full speed ahead!" exclaimed Captain David Glasgow Farragut during the Civil War battle of Mobile Bay. Farragut was the naval hero of the Union during the Civil War. To honor him, Congress created the rank of admiral in 1866.

Farragut was born at Stony Point, near Knoxville, Tennessee. He was adopted by a naval officer after his mother died. He became a midshipman in the Navy when he was only nine years old. In those days, the U.S. Naval Academy did not exist, and naval officers were trained at sea. He took part in attacks on British ships during the War of 1812 and fought pirates in the West Indies during the 1820s. He became a commander in 1841 and a captain in 1855.

Although he was a southerner, Farragut took the side of the North in the Civil War. He was given command of a Union (northern) fleet and was ordered to blockade southern ports in the Gulf of Mexico. The blockade severely hindered the South from getting vital supplies and from sending its cotton to the markets of Europe. Farragut and his fleet captured New Orleans in April, 1862, after a hard battle.

Farragut fought his greatest battle at Mobile Bay in August, 1864. The city of Mobile, Alabama, was protected by gunboats,

David Farragut, brave naval officer who fought on the Union side during the Civil War.

A salamander is a small lizard that can dart about quickly to avoid danger. Farragut moved his ships so fast out of enemy fire during the Civil War that he earned the name "Old Salamander."

forts, and underwater mines called "torpedoes." Farragut led his fleet into the bay. An officer warned him about the torpedoes. It was then that Farragut gave the order that has become so well known. A fierce battle took place. Farragut and his ships won. The city of Mobile surrendered a few days later.

ALSO READ: CIVIL WAR, NAVY.

FASCISM The word "fascism" comes from the Latin word *fasces,* describing a bundle of rods which enclose an ax. The blade of the ax sticks up above the rods. A red cord holds the rods around the ax. The fasces were carried ahead of ancient Roman officials as a symbol of power. The rods represent the power of punishment. The ax stands for the power over life and death. This ancient symbol of power has been used to represent the power of the fascist state over its people.

In a fascist state, the people must be absolutely loyal to the country and its government. The individual person must sacrifice his personal needs and wishes for the "collective good," or the good of the entire society. The "state" is supreme.

A fascist state is usually controlled by one person (a dictator) who, in turn, controls the only existing political party. The party members are a small group of people who believe themselves to be superior to all other people, and therefore entitled to control or destroy anyone whom they consider to be inferior. They want everyone to share their ideas and to work hard for certain goals. Those people who do not support them or who even mildly disagree with them are severely punished. Fascists blame their own failures on various groups of people. The fascists of Nazi Germany killed millions of Jews, gypsies, and members of other minority groups for this reason.

A fascist government has complete power over all the activities of its country, from what is printed in newspapers to what is taught in schools. Benito Mussolini and his political party had such control in Italy between 1922 and 1943. Germany was also a fascist state from 1933 to 1945, under the dictatorship of Adolf Hitler and his Nazi party. The German fascist government was *totalitarian*—it tried to control everything that the people did or thought. Anyone who did not obey was punished. Fascist governments have also existed in Asia, Central and South America, and Spain.

How do fascists manage to acquire such power? Usually the conditions in the country are bad. There is much unemployment and most people do not have enough money to buy the things they need. Sometimes the fascist party starts a campaign of writings and speeches criticizing the existing government and telling the people that they are a superior nation and deserve better things. The fascists promise a glorious future for their nation. The people believe them and, desiring a better life, they often give fascists power by voting for them! Once they are in control, the fascists try to make the people think that they have a part in the government by holding elections and political meetings. But the elections and meetings are controlled, and the people have no real control over national affairs. Fascist governments may attempt to gain more land for their "superior" citizens to settle in—even if they must go to war to do this. Germany's desire for more "living room" was a major cause of World War II.

ALSO READ: DICTATOR; GERMAN HISTORY; GOVERNMENT; HITLER, ADOLF; ITALIAN HISTORY; MUSSOLINI, BENITO; SPANISH HISTORY; WORLD WAR II.

FASHION   When many people start dressing a certain way, or buying a certain article of furniture or decoration, it has become a fashion. Changes in clothing fashions are usually the most obvious. People used to think that the custom of clothing the body began because of modesty (wanting to hide the body). But now it is thought that the main reason for the first clothing—aside from protection from weather—was to make oneself more attractive.

Clothing in the ancient countries of Egypt, Greece, and Rome was extremely simple in form, even among the rich. Egyptians wore little clothing because of the warm climate in Egypt. Clothing they did wear was of cotton or linen, the coolest materials. Both men and women—as in most hot climates—wore skirted instead of trousered clothing, either short or long. Their jewelry, however, was rich and elaborate and was worn on many parts of the body.

Early Greeks wore clothing of materials having designs woven into them. But, when the city-state of Athens became leader of Greece, everyone started using the plain white material worn by Athenians. Fashions have very often been set in this way by countries that led or conquered other countries.

Greeks and Romans draped or wrapped cloth around the body rather than cutting and fitting it. The common Roman clothing for male citizens was the *toga*, a cloth wound around the body and covering one shoulder. The border or pattern on it indicated rank or office. Women wore a long, flowing dress, the *stola*. Under the outer garments both men and women wore tunics.

Early medieval Europeans continued to wear unfitted clothing—chiefly a tunic or two tunics, and cloaks. Men also wore tights. Floor-length robes were worn by both sexes. The biggest fashion change of this period occurred in the mid-1400s, when people began wearing clothes fitted to the body. Coats and vests were first worn by men about 1660.

▲Ancient Egyptians wore loose skirted clothing.

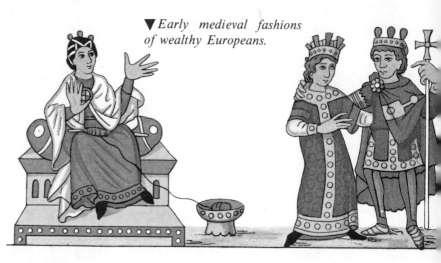

▲The traditional Japanese kimono has been worn for centuries.

fashions through the ages

▼Early medieval fashions of wealthy Europeans.

▲A court page of the Middle Ages wearing a belted tunic with wide loose sleeves and tights.

▼A French king and queen during the middle 1500s set the fashions of the day.

▲Clothing of the Revolutionary War period in the United States.

▲A young European girl in a pretty dress about 1800.

▲The long, sleek look was fashion news in the 1930s.

▲Fashion influenced the clothes of airline stewardesses in the 1960s.

◄Anything goes with the fashions of the 1970s, including bell-bottoms and mini-to-maxi dress lengths.

▶The clothing industry employs attractive models to show off the latest designs. The models help to sell fashion to the public.

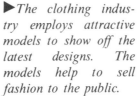

Lace decorations worn around the neck (called ruffs) were very popular during the reign of Queen Elizabeth I. Ruffs grew so large that people had to use spoons with extra-long handles to avoid crushing their ruffs while eating.

Women continued to wear robes till about the 1500s, when they started wearing full, tight-waisted skirts held out from the body by a set of hoops of whalebone, called the *farthingale*. After this period, European styles began changing faster. Fashion change often goes along with changes in the world. Explorers were visiting faraway lands at this period. Europeans were visiting each other's countries more often. More people were living in large towns. They had more money to spend, and they met large numbers of people, unlike people of earlier times who lived in small villages all their lives.

New fabrics, such as silk brought back by explorers from China, began to be used. Brocade, which was made from silk, and velvet were worn by the wealthy.

Some styles were begun by famous people, such as King Louis XIV of France. He began wearing extremely fancy silks, laces, and high heels, and he made his court gentlemen do the same. With these, he made himself and the crown seem more important. The clothing was a symbol of power and grandeur that everyone could see.

Popular writers influenced fashion even before mass communication. The French philosopher Jean Jacques Rousseau wrote about the goodness of simple country life. Queen Marie Antoinette of France and her court ladies began to wear simple cotton gowns after reading his novels and essays.

Certain countries have gained popularity in the eyes of others and thus influenced fashion. Empress Catherine the Great of Russia visited France and returned home telling of her admiration for French life and culture. The Russian upper classes adopted French clothing, as well as the French language.

Clothing fashions have often been a way of expressing political views or even a whole way of looking at life. The plain, unchanging dress of English Puritans (some of the first European immigrants to America), the American Quakers, and some of the stricter Amish groups of Pennsylvania showed their belief that clothes were unimportant as decoration, and further, that material goods were not very important to life.

Uncomfortable clothing, or clothing that makes it difficult to move around, can show that the wearers are rich enough to live lives of ease. Hoop skirts, which were worn from the 1600s through much of the 1700s, were an example of this.

In the 1800s, men's clothing, at least, became more comfortable. Instead of knee-length, tight breeches, men began wearing long trousers allowing for more movement. The "lounge suit," much like today's business suit, began to be worn. This suit, and the more formal tailcoat, were adapted from sporting clothes, rather than from court dress (formal wear).

Women's clothes continued to be stiff, full-skirted, tight-waisted, and over-decorated all through the 1800s and early

1900s. The one exception was around the time when Napoleon was Emperor of France and encouraged "Empire" styles like those of Greece and Rome. The "empire" waistline (above the natural waist) and loose, flowing dresses were popular then.

Corsets were worn under the stiff styles of women's dress. They were often fastened so tightly that women fainted—if women were fashionable enough to want an artificially tiny waistline.

Clothing for women became more loose and comfortable during and after World War I (1914–1918). The 1920s began a complete change in female clothing. Corsets were no longer worn, and hemlines went up and up. This change took place after a great change in attitude toward women. Part of it was caused by women's starting to work outside the home. They had to have greater ease of movement in their clothing.

Another big change in fashion in the 1900s was the adoption of more fashionable clothes by a larger group of people. Mass production of clothing made it possible for people to buy cheaper clothes that were stylish. Before this, a huge division existed between the wealthy, whose styles changed with the season, and the poor, who wore the same style year after year.

Today, when many people travel, and television and newspapers go all over the world, clothing styles have spread to countries where, formerly, an unchanging national costume was worn.

Fashion changes today seem fast from our point of view. But small changes—which make the clothes of 1960, for example, seem "out of fashion"—will not seem so important to people looking back at us centuries from now.

Probably one of the changes or trends of today that is important is *unisex* clothing style ("uni" means "one"). Not since early medieval days have men and women tried to look alike in clothing style. A second important change is the wearing of extremely comfortable, informal clothing, even in places where people would formerly have worn stiff, formal dress. As with other fashions, these have followed from new ideas about the roles of men and women, and from the more informal and comfortable ways people today speak, behave, and live.

ALSO READ: CLOTHING, FEATHER, HAT, JEWELRY, KNITTING, LACE, SEWING, SHOES.

FATES Three goddesses in ancient Greek and Roman myths were called the *Fates.* They were in charge of the thread of life. The Greeks named them the *Moirai. Clotho's* job was to spin the thread of life. *Lachesis* decided how long the thread should be, and *Atropos* cut it with her shears. The Roman name for the Fates was *Parcae,* and their individual names were *Nona, Decuma,* and *Morta.*

Men did not want to die and, according to the myth, they

▲*The Three Fates, who were thought to decide how long men should live.*

begged the Fates to stop spinning and cutting. Men gave the Fates rich gifts and pleaded with them for longer life. But the stern, unbending Fates worked on, never heeding. There were Fates in many other mythologies as well, including the Norse and Indian.

ALSO READ: GODS AND GODDESSES, MYTHOLOGY.

FATHERS OF CONFEDERATION Most of the British colonies in North America revolted against England in 1775 and formed the United States. But north of the U.S., six British colonies still remained. They were Canada East (now Quebec), Canada West (now Ontario), New Brunswick, Nova Scotia, Prince Edward Island, and Newfoundland. The Fathers of Confederation were 33 delegates from these remaining colonies who met at Quebec in 1864 to plan the creation of a united and in-

FATHERS OF CONFEDERATION	REGION
Adams G. Archibald	Nova Scotia
George Brown	Canada West
Alexander Campbell	Canada West
Frederick Bowker T. Carter	Newfoundland
George Etienne Cartier	Canada East
Edward B. Chandler	New Brunswick
Jean-Charles Chapais	Canada East
James Cockburn	Canada West
George Coles	Prince Edward Island
Robert B. Dickey	Nova Scotia
Charles Fisher	New Brunswick
Alexander T. Galt	Canada East
Col. John Hamilton Gray	Prince Edward Island
John Hamilton Gray	New Brunswick
Thomas H. Haviland	Prince Edward Island
William A. Henry	Nova Scotia
William P. Howland*	Canada West
John M. Johnson	New Brunswick
Hector-Louis Langevin	Canada East
Jonathan McCully	Nova Scotia
Andrew A. Macdonald	Prince Edward Island
John A. Macdonald	Canada West
William McDougall	Canada West
T. D'Arcy McGee	Canada East
Peter Mitchell	New Brunswick
Oliver Mowat	Canada West
Edward Palmer	Prince Edward Island
William H. Pope	Prince Edward Island
John W. Ritchie*	Nova Scotia
Ambrose Shea	Newfoundland
William H. Steeves	New Brunswick
Étienne-Paschal Taché	Canada East
S. Leonard Tilley	New Brunswick
Charles Tupper	Nova Scotia
Edward Whelan	Prince Edward Island
Robert D. Wilmot*	New Brunswick

Canada East is now Quebec. Canada West is now Ontario.
*Not among original 33, but helped win
British approval in 1866.

dependent country. The result of their work was the formation of the Dominion of Canada in 1867. All the colonies, except Prince Edward Island and Newfoundland, joined the new confederation.

The most colorful father of the confederation was Sir John A. Macdonald (1815–1891), who became the first prime minister of the new country. He was born in Glasgow, Scotland. His family could afford to send him to school for only a few years. But Macdonald found a job in a lawyer's office in Canada and soon began to practice law himself. He entered politics before he was 30.

Macdonald's closest friend was George Cartier (1814–1873), a French-Canadian. It was largely due to Cartier's efforts that the French-speaking people of Quebec agreed to join their English-speaking neighbors and form a single country.

The stormiest father of the confederation was George Brown (1818–1880), a journalist and politician also born in Scotland. Unlike Macdonald, he received a strong formal education. He moved to Toronto and set about making the Liberal Party the chief rival of Macdonald's Conservatives. The newspaper he founded, now called the *Globe and Mail*, remains Canada's most important daily paper.

The Fathers of Confederation had many different ideas, but they shared one dream. They wanted to create a new North American country that would stretch from coast to coast. These men had the determination to make this dream come true.

ALSO READ: CANADA; MACDONALD, JOHN A.

FATS AND OILS Animals and plants may eat or absorb more food than they need to keep alive and provide energy for the things they do. Living things store most of the extra food in their bodies as *fats* and *oils*. These substances can be stored because they do not dissolve in water, which is part of all living cells. Plants usually store fats and oils in seeds. Animals store fats and oils in all the tissues of their bodies.

Both fats and oils are made up of carbon, hydrogen, and oxygen, which form compounds called *glycerides*. The main difference between fats and oils is that, at ordinary temperatures, fats are solids and oils are liquids. (The oil that comes from oil wells is a very different substance from the fats and oils that come from plants and animals.)

Fats and oils are reserve materials that a living thing can use from its own body when its food supply does not provide enough fuel. A ground squirrel makes good use of fat. In late summer and autumn, the ground squirrel stuffs himself with food. In winter, little food is available, so the ground squirrel hibernates (sleeps all winter). Its heart needs energy to keep beating. Its lungs need energy to breathe. This energy comes

▼ *Many foods are fried in fat or oil. One of the most popular dishes in the U.S. is ham and eggs.*

from the fat the animal stored up in autumn. In spring, when the ground squirrel wakes from its long sleep, it is skinny because all its extra fat was used up.

Fats, proteins, and carbohydrates are the three main classes of foods. Fats (and oils) provide more than twice as much energy for the body to use as either proteins or carbohydrates. Most fats contain vitamins A and D. Vitamin D prevents the bone disease called rickets. Vitamin A is necessary for growth.

Fats and oils are also important in industry. Fats, especially plant fats, are the basic ingredient of soap. Animal fat, called *tallow,* is used in candle making. And fats are necessary in making drugs, paints, lubricants, waxes, and polishes, as well as many other products.

Some familiar fats are butter, oleomargarine, and lard. Some common oils are olive, cottonseed, palm, coconut, peanut, linseed, cod-liver, and castor.

ALSO READ: CHEMISTRY, HIBERNATION, NUTRITION, PETROLEUM.

▲*Faust is tempted to sell his soul to the devil, a frontispiece from* Life and Death of Dr. Faustus *written by Christopher Marlowe about 1589.*

FAUST, JOHANN A man named Georg Faustus lived in Germany during the early 1500s. He was a magician and fortune teller, and his tricks were so clever that people began to tell strange stories about him. The stories continued after Faustus died and, somehow, he began to be called Johann Faust. The basic story, or legend, said that Faust traded his soul to the devil in return for 24 years of magic powers. Other stories gave "examples" of his powers.

During the more than 400 years since Faustus died, many people have been fascinated by his legend. Christopher Marlowe (an English poet), the great German author Goethe, and many other writers have used the Faust legend in their works. Goethe changed the story to allow Faust to save himself. Charles Gounod, a French composer, wrote the music for a popular opera called *Faust* (1859). Other composers have also told Faust's story in music.

ALSO READ: LEGEND, LITERATURE, MUSIC, OPERA.

▼*Guy Fawkes plotting with his fellow conspirators to blow up the British Parliament.*

FAWKES, GUY (1570–1606) Bonfires and fireworks blaze all over England every year on November 5, Guy Fawkes Day. Children make dummies called "guys" (or dress up as "guys") and go from house to house begging "a penny for the guy."

On November 5, 1605, Guy Fawkes was arrested for plotting to blow up the king and his government in Parliament. The "Gunpowder Plot" was discovered, and the English still celebrate the capture of Guy Fawkes.

Guy Fawkes was born in York, England. He became an ardent Roman Catholic. He joined the army of the Catholic king of Spain as a young man. By the time Fawkes returned to England, the Protestant king, James I, and his Parliament had

passed harsh laws against the practice of the Catholic religion. Guy Fawkes and a group of Catholic friends plotted to blow up the king and the Parliament. They dug a tunnel into the basement under the meeting room of Parliament's House of Lords. But someone warned a member of the House of Lords to stay away from Parliament on November 5. The member of the House of Lords warned the other members. Soldiers searched the basement and found Fawkes guarding 36 barrels of gunpowder. Fawkes and the other members of his group were put to death.

ALSO READ: ENGLISH HISTORY.

A traditional English rhyme about Guy Fawkes goes:
Please to remember the fifth of November,
Gunpowder treason and plot.
There is no reason why such treason
Should ever be forgot.

◀ *The male peafowl, or peacock, has beautiful iridescent, or rainbow-like, colored feathers. The peacock spreads its long tail feathers like a fan to attract the female peahen.*

FEATHER Have you ever heard someone say, "Like water off a duck's back"? What is so special about a duck's back? The backs of ducks (and all birds) are covered with *feathers.* Not only do these feathers keep birds warm and dry, but some feathers also help them swim! *Powder-down feathers* have ends that dry up and disintegrate, leaving a dry, waxy powder that spreads over the rest of the plumage. This waxy powder protects the feathers from water, causing the water to form "beads" and slide off, and adds to the bird's buoyancy when swimming!

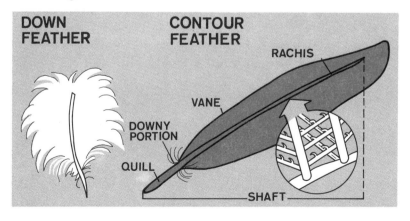

DOWN FEATHER

CONTOUR FEATHER

RACHIS

VANE

DOWNY PORTION

QUILL

SHAFT

◀ *The* vane, *or flat part, of* a contour feather is made of *an intricate mass of* barbs hooked together.

▲*Contour feathers of a roller bird showing the quill and rachis of the shaft.*

There are two kinds of feathers. *Contour* feathers extend outward from the wings and tail, and are an important part of the bird's flight system. *Down* feathers are soft, silky feathers under the contour feathers. Down feathers provide warmth.

Feathers have been used by man in three principal ways. Before the invention of steel pens, most writing was done with *quill* pens. These are large contour feathers that have a sharpened quill (hard, hollow center) and a split point, which is dipped in ink for writing.

Feathers have also been used to stuff pillows, quilts, and upholstery. With the invention of synthetic (man-made) stuffings, feather-stuffed objects are no longer common. But they are still considered the most comfortable and most expensive stuffing available.

Since prehistoric times, feathers have formed part of the decorative dress of man. The North American Indians used eagle feathers in their headdress for identification. The position of the feather or the angle at which it was worn indicated the tribe of the wearer. In Europe and America, feathers have long been used by both men and women to decorate various parts of their clothing, including fans, hats, and capes.

The demand in the United States and elsewhere for feathers to be used for ornamentation led to great slaughter of birds and the extinction or near-extinction of several species. Many societies have been formed to promote the passage of laws restricting the killing of birds for their feathers. The most famous of these is the National Association of Audubon Societies.

ALSO READ: AUDUBON, JOHN JAMES; BIRD; CLOTHING; PENS AND PENCILS.

FEBRUARY The first Roman calendar had only ten months, and February was not among them. Numa Pompilius, a legendary king of Rome, is supposed to have added January as the eleventh month and February as the twelfth month. The name February comes from the Latin word *februare,* which means "to purify." It was the Romans' custom to purify themselves for the beginning of the new year. Later, Julius Caesar set up a new calendar. He moved the start of the year from March to January, and February became the second month. February has 28 days, except in *leap years,* when it has 29 days. Leap years occur every four years.

Americans celebrate many days in February. George Washington and Abraham Lincoln were both born in this month. Valentine's Day comes on the fourteenth. Ground-hog Day is February 2. Some people believe that if the ground hog (woodchuck) comes out of his burrow and sees his shadow, winter will last for six more weeks. If he sees no shadow, spring will come soon. Each year, you can learn the ground hog's "weather

DATES OF SPECIAL EVENTS IN FEBRUARY

1 • Supreme Court of the U.S. met for the first time (1790).
  • Feast of Saint Brigid, or Bridget, beloved saint of Ireland.
2 • Treaty of Guadalupe Hidalgo signed. Mexico ceded New Mexico and California to the U.S. (1848).
  • James Joyce, great Irish novelist, was born (1882).
  • Candlemas, a Christian festival, to honor the Virgin Mary.
  • Ground-hog Day. According to myth, if the sun is shining and the ground hog can see its shadow, there will be six more weeks of winter weather.
3 • Felix Mendelssohn, German composer, was born (1809).
  • Horace Greeley, American publisher, was born (1811).
4 • Confederate States of America formed in Montgomery, Alabama (1861).
  • Charles Lindbergh, American aviator, was born (1902).
6 • Babe Ruth, great major league baseball player, was born (1895).
7 • Charles Dickens, English writer, was born (1812).
  • Sinclair Lewis, American writer, was born (1885).
8 • Jules Verne, French writer, was born (1828).
  • Boy Scout Day, celebrated by Boy Scouts of America, commemorating the incorporation of the organization in the U.S. in 1910.
9 • President William Henry Harrison was born (1773).
10 • France ceded Canada to Great Britain (1763).
11 • Thomas A. Edison, American inventor, was born (1847).
12 • President Abraham Lincoln was born (1809).
  • Charles Darwin, English scientist, was born (1809).
14 • Valentine's Day, the Feast of Saint Valentine, when people send cards of greeting to people they like.
15 • Galileo, Italian astronomer, was born (1564).
  • The battleship U.S.S. *Maine* exploded in the harbor of Havana, Cuba (1898).
  • Festival of San Isidro de Coronado in the town of that name in Costa Rica. Painted oxcarts parade through the streets.
18 • Jefferson Davis became provisional president of the Confederate States (1861).
19 • Nicolaus Copernicus, Polish astronomer, was born (1473).
  Edison patented his phonograph (1878).
20 • John Glenn, first U.S. astronaut in orbit, orbited Earth three times (1962).
22 • President George Washington was born (1732).
  • Frederic Chopin, Polish pianist and composer, was born (1810).
  • Spain ceded Florida to the U.S. (1819).
  • Robert Baden-Powell, founder of the Boy Scouts, was born (1857).
23 • George Frederick Handel, English composer, was born in Germany (1633).
25 • An income tax was set up by amendment of the Constitution—16th Amendment (1913).
26 • Buffalo Bill was born (1846).
28 • Vincent Massey became the first governor-general of Canada born in Canada (1952).

forecast" by observing the weather on February 2. If the sun is shining, the ground hog will certainly see his shadow. Check to see if his "guess" is correct.

February's flower is the violet, and the purple amethyst is its birthstone.

ALSO READ: CALENDAR, HOLIDAY, MONTH.

▶*A scientist employed by the FBI examines some clothing to see if stains on it were made by blood.*

FEDERAL BUREAU OF INVESTIGATION The Bureau of Investigation was founded in 1908 as a section of the U.S. Department of Justice. "Federal" was added to its name in 1935, officially making it the Federal Bureau of Investigation (FBI). The job of the FBI is to gather information about (investigate) federal crimes. The FBI does not investigate *counterfeiting* (making imitation money) or violations of drug, tax, postal, or customs laws. The FBI does not take people to court. That is the job of the Attorney General or the police departments, to whom the FBI gives information.

John Edgar Hoover became director of the Bureau in 1924, when he was 29. He served until his death in 1972. During that period, the FBI became one of the most important law enforcement agencies in the world.

The FBI has headquarters in Washington, D.C., and offices in cities throughout the United States. It cooperates with police to solve many local crimes. It gathers information about federal crimes, such as civil rights violations and aircraft hijacking; about law suits involving the United States government; and about crimes that involve more than one state. The FBI also investigates crimes of espionage (spying) and kidnapping. For reasons of national security, it keeps files on people and organizations important to the Federal Government. Because of these records, the FBI is often accused of "snooping"—investigating people's private lives unnecessarily. The FBI has the largest collection of fingerprints in the world. It also has a modern criminal laboratory, where scientists examine evidence sent from law enforcement offices across the nation.

The special agents of the FBI are usually graduates of law or accounting schools. They undergo rigorous training at the FBI National Academy in Washington, D.C. Other law enforcement officers from the U.S. and abroad also take this training.
ALSO READ: DETECTIVE, FINGERPRINT, POLICE, UNITED STATES GOVERNMENT.

The FBI publishes the "Most Wanted List" of persons it especially wants to capture. The people on the list are considered dangerous to society. The FBI often asks the public to help find these people.